Travel
Guidebooks
in Review

TRAVEL GUIDEBOOKS IN REVIEW

Third Edition, Revised

Edited by JON O. HEISE
        Director of the International Center
        University of Michigan

and by Lynn Gumpert, Jon V.C. Booth, & Susan I. Nisbett

1978

GAYLORD
PROFESSIONAL
PUBLICATIONS
Syracuse, NY, 13221

© The University of Michigan 1974, 1975, 1978
Originally published under the title *Suit Your Spirit*
by the International Center of the University of Michigan
This third edition completely revised
and the title changed

Published and distributed by
Gaylord Professional Publications
Syracuse, New York 13221

Library of Congress Cataloging in Publication Data

Main entry under title:

Travel guidebooks in review.

Second ed. (c1975) published under title:
Suit your spirit.
Bibliography: p.
Includes index.
1. Voyages and travels—1951-   —Guide-
books—Bibliography. I. Heise, Jon O.
II. Suit your spirit.
Z6016.T7S9 1978 [G153]   016.91'02   78-16930
ISBN 0-915794-25-X

Printed in the United States of America

Contents

PREFACE	11
INTRODUCTION	13
KEY TO SYMBOLS	18

PART 1. EUROPE

Introduction 21

Annually Revised Guides

1	Europe on $10 a Day	25
2	Fielding's Low-Cost Europe	26
3	Fielding's Travel Guide to Europe	27
4	Fodor's Europe	29
5	Let's Go: The Budget Guide to Europe	30
6	Myra Waldo's Travel and Motoring Guide to Europe	31

TRAVEL GUIDEBOOKS

Specialty Guides

7	Fielding's Guide to Traveling with Children in Europe	35
8	The Special Guide to Europe	36
9	Traveler's Guide Book to Europe and Asia: Your Passport to Making It Abroad	37
10	The Traveller's Survival Kit: Europe	39
11	Whitman's Off Season Travel Guide to Europe	40
12	Youth Hosteler's Guide to Europe	41

Series Guides about Specific Countries, Cities, or Regions

13	A to Z World Travel Guides	45
14	Arthur Frommer's Guides	46
15	Berlitz Travel Guides	48
16	Blue Guides	50
17	Dollar Wise Guides	52
18	Fodor's Guides	53
19	Holiday Travel Guides	56
20	Michelin Green Guides (English Editions)	57
21	Nagel's Encyclopedia-Guides	59
22	Sunset Travel Guides	61
23	$10-A-Day Guides	62

Accommodation and Restaurant Guides

24	AA Budget Guide to Europe	67
25	AAA European Accommodations	68
26	Castle Hotels of Europe	69
27	Country Inns and Back Roads, European Edition	70
28	Fielding's Selected Favorites: Hotels and Inns, Europe	71
29	International Youth Hostel Handbook: Volume I, Europe and Mediterranean Countries	72
30	Michelin Red Guides	73
31	Student Hostels and Tour Activities: Handbook for the Young Traveler	74

Train Guides

32	Baxter's Eurailpass Travel Guide	79
33	Enjoy Europe by Train	80
34	Eurail Guide: How to Travel Europe by Train	81
35	Europe by Eurail	82

Motoring and Camping Guides

36	AA Guide to Camping and Caravaning on the Continent	87
37	AA Guide to Continental Motoring	88
38	AAA Travel Guide to Europe	89
39	Enjoy Europe by Car	90
40	Europa Camping and Caravaning	91
41	Europa Touring: Motoring Guide of Europe	93
42	European Camping and Caravaning	94
43	How to Camp Europe by Train	95
44	Motor Camping Around Europe	96
45	Rand McNally European Campground Guide	97

Bicycling and Walking Guides

46	Bicycle Touring in Europe	101
47	Turn Right at the Fountain	102
48	Walk Straight Through the Square and More Walk Straight Through the Square	103
49	Wandering: A Walker's Guide to the Mountain Trails of Europe	104

PART 2. AFRICA

Introduction		109
50	Africa for the Hitchhiker	111
51	Africa Guide	112
51A	Africa on the Cheap	113
52	Africa on Wheels: A Scrounger's Guide to Motoring in Africa	115

8   TRAVEL GUIDEBOOKS

53	Bright Continent: A Shoestring Guide to Sub-Saharan Africa	116
54	East Africa: A Travel Guide	117
55	The Traveler's Africa	119

PART 3. ASIA

Introduction 123

56	Across Asia on the Cheap	125
57	All-Asia Guide	126
58	Fodor's Southeast Asia	127
59	Myra Waldo's Travel Guide to the Orient and the Pacific	129
60	The On-Your-Own Guide to Asia	130
61	Pacific Paradise on a Low Budget	131
62	South-East Asia on a Shoestring	132
63	The Student Guide to Asia	133

PART 4. SOUTH AMERICA

Introduction 137

64	Fodor's South America	139
65	Myra Waldo's Travel Guide to South America	140
66	South America on $10 and $15 a Day	141
67	The South American Handbook	142
68	The Student Guide to Latin America	143

PART 5. WORLDWIDE

Introduction 147

69	Ford's Freighter Travel Guide and Ford's International Cruise Guide	149
70	Fodor's Cruises Everywhere, 1977	150
71	Fodor's Railways of the World	151
72	The Freighter Travel Manual	152

73	How to Travel Without Being Rich	154
74	Off the Beaten Track: A Wexas Travel Handbook	155
75	Overlanding: How to Explore the World on Four Wheels	157
76	Pan Am's World Guide: The Encyclopedia of Travel	158
77	Rand McNally Traveler's Almanac: The International Guide	159
78	Whole World Handbook: A Student Guide to Work, Study and Travel Abroad	160

APPENDIXES
I	Alphabetical List of All Books	165
II	Names and Addresses of All Publishers and Distributors of Books Reviewed	168
III	Guidebooks Published in Series	175
IV	Basic Travel Library	182
V	Basic Study Abroad Library	184
VI	Basic International Employment Library	186

Preface

Over the years, we at the University of Michigan International Center have received hundreds of inquiries from students about the "best" guidebook to take along when traveling. In order to answer this perennial question, we decided to seek answers in a systematic way. Thus began our review of guidebooks on a standard format basis.

As members of the National Association of Foreign Student Affairs, we were also aware that others in the low-cost and student travel field were in need of the same information, as were libraries and bookstores. Given the needs of both ourselves and others, we decided to publish our results in the first edition of *Travel Guidebooks in Review* in 1973 (then titled *Suit Your Spirit*).

The book is intended to meet the needs of advisors of students and low-cost travelers—those who assist individuals in planning and experiencing enjoyable, effective, and inexpensive travel. It may be used as a reference tool for the traveler and as a resource for the librarian, bookseller, or other person assisting in travel information.

Enormous credit must be given to Lynn Gumpert, who wrote the majority of the reviews contained in this volume. Her organizational abilities and writing skills have made this book possible. Editorial skills were also provided by Jon V.C. Booth and Susan I. Nisbett, both of whom have contributed greatly to the production of this book.

Travel Guidebooks in Review has been developed in each of its editions by the University of Michigan International Center, which is responsible to the Office of Student Services, reporting through the Office of Student Programs.

JON O. HEISE

Ann Arbor, Michigan, 1978

Introduction

WHY *Travel Guidebooks in Review*
WAS WRITTEN

Over the last two decades, the profile of the international traveler has changed. More people with limited budgets venture abroad often seeking an in-depth travel experience. Travel guides have expanded in number and in scope to meet this growing and changing audience.

Recognizing the need for an overview of the available travel literature, this book steers prospective readers to the guidebooks that best fit their needs. Because the work reviews a wide variety of travel options, it will be helpful to readers in defining their travel goals.

WHAT'S INCLUDED

Seventy-eight travel guidebooks and series of

guidebooks have been selected for review in this publication, according to certain priorities.

Limited- or *modest-budget* travel books are the special focus of *Travel Guidebooks in Review*.

Classic or *well-established* guides are also included. These may deal with a type of travel out of reach of the limited-budget traveler but are among the best-known and most frequently found guides.

Hard-to-find specialty books have been included when they excel in a particular area. Since these are often not available in local bookstores, information is provided on purchase by mail.

What's Not Included

Guides not revised in the last three years are not included unless they provide unique or outstanding information not available elsewhere.

Country and city guides have not been included. The only exception to this is guides published in series. In these cases, the series as a whole is reviewed rather than the individual guides. A listing of the books by series is found in appendix III.

North American guides have not been included.

Accuracy of Information

Every effort has been made to ascertain whether the books reviewed in this edition would remain in print. It must be noted, however, that the editors of this volume are not responsible for any subsequent changes in price, type of edition, mergers of organizations, address changes, or other unforseen changes.

How To Use This Book

In using this book, it is necessary that you first select the geographic area you wish to visit. Then turn to the chapter covering that area. An introduction will provide essential information on the type of travel guides available.

Each travel guide is reviewed according to a set format, designed to facilitate comparison between guides. The title, author(s), place of publication, publisher, price, style of publication, number of pages, and year of publication are listed at the top of the review. For books not published in the United States, addresses of U.S. distributors are provided for purchase by mail. All other books are available from local bookstores or the publisher (see appendix II for addresses of all publishers). Three sections follow:

(1) *Purpose and Audience:* This section summarizes the kind of people to whom the guide is directed, the areas and countries covered, and the purpose of the guide.

(2) *What's included:* Using symbols, this section conveys the major topics covered by the guide. If the coverage is especially thorough, a circle is placed around the symbol. A key to the symbols can be found on page 18.

(3) *Evaluation:* Evaluations of a guide are based on how well it lives up to the goals it sets for itself and how well the material is organized.

Certain specific terms have been used to describe various budget categories. It will be useful to the reader to be familiar with these terms prior to reading the reviews.

Rock Bottom indicates the very lowest possible budget for traveling and usually indicates hitchhiking or camping as the style of travel.

Low applies to people who may wish to combine stays in low-cost hotels or hostels with discount train and air fares.

Moderate implies an average limited budget. Low prices are a concern but not an absolute criterion. Travelers with moderate budgets, as we define them, are able to afford travel experiences suggested in *Fielding's Low-Cost Europe* and *Fodor's Europe*.

These categories are not rigid and will differ slightly from region to region. Check area introductions for more specific definitions.

How to Use the Appendixes

There are six appendixes to help you find information quickly.

Appendix I
  Alphabetical List of All Books
Appendix II
  Names and Addresses of All Publishers and Distributors of Books Reviewed
Appendix III
  Guidebooks Published in Series
 If you enjoy Fodor guidebooks, for example, this section will let you know the areas of the world about which Fodor's publishes books.
Appendix IV
  Basic Travel Library
Appendix V
  Basic Study Abroad Library
Appendix VI
  Basic International Employment Library

The last three appendixes are especially designed for librarians and university international offices that wish to establish a basic library of books.

How to Choose a Travel Guide

Prior to selecting a guidebook, you should decide where you want to go and what you want out of your trip. You can get some ideas by spending some time glancing at reviews contained in this book. When you have made these basic decisions, you are ready to begin looking for specific books that meet your purposes most closely. Books included have been chosen for their ability to help you save both time and money while getting the most out of your travels.

Here are some points you might want to consider:

(1) Who is the author? Has he or she lived in a country or just traveled there? If it is a book in a series, does the same person write all the books or are area specialists selected to write the guides to specific countries?

(2) Check out the suggested wardrobe for traveling. This will often indicate to you whether the author's lifestyle (and travel style) is roughly compatible with your own.

(3) Check the publication or revision date. Much travel material becomes out of date quickly. For accommodations and restaurant suggestions and, even more important, price information and passport and visa regulations, up-to-date information is of prime concern.

(4) Don't reject a guide because it doesn't provide all the information you consider vital. Consider taking along parts of various books or combining a general accommodations/restaurant guide with a guide to the history, culture, or sights of an area.

(5) Check for guides *during* your travels. Occasionally you can find a gem that is not available in the United States.

A Final Note

A travel guide shouldn't limit or cramp your style. It can be as flexibile as you are. You needn't stick to only those hotels or restaurants suggested. In fact, many excellent books suggest guidelines for getting beyond the traditional, tourist-oriented routes and exploring on your own.

A good guide can be an additional "friend," bailing you out of a difficult situation by giving you that necessary address or suggesting an all-night restaurant. A good trav-

18 TRAVEL GUIDEBOOKS

eler is one who is open to learning; a good guidebook provides otherwise inaccessible information. They go hand in hand.

KEY TO SYMBOLS FOR TRAVEL GUIDEBOOKS IN REVIEW

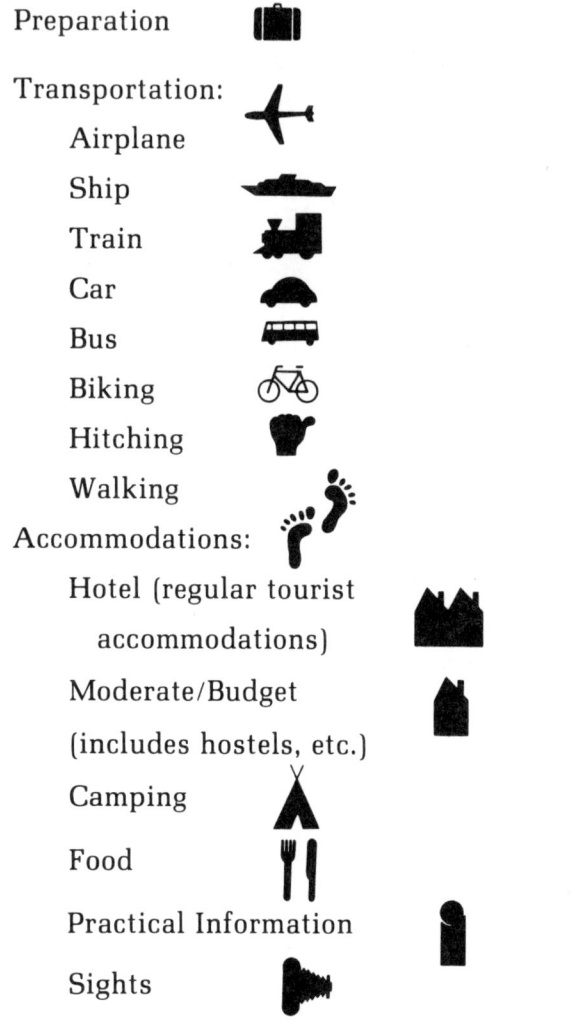

Preparation

Transportation:
    Airplane
    Ship
    Train
    Car
    Bus
    Biking
    Hitching
    Walking

Accommodations:
    Hotel (regular tourist accommodations)
    Moderate/Budget (includes hostels, etc.)
    Camping
    Food
    Practical Information
    Sights

A circle around the symbol denotes especially complete coverage.

Part One

Europe

Introduction

An incredible variety of guides is now available for travel in Europe. Concurrent with the increase in European travel has come the appearance of specialized travel guides. We have organized the European guides into the following subchapters:

(1) ANNUALLY REVISED GUIDES: These are survey, "Grand Tour" approach guides to all of Europe. All are readily available at most bookstores.

(2) SPECIALTY GUIDES: These are general travel guides that, like the annually revised guides, cover all of Europe, but with a special focus (for example, *Fielding's Guide to Traveling with Children in Europe*).

(3) SERIES GUIDES ABOUT SPECIFIC COUNTRIES, CITIES, OR REGIONS: Each series has been reviewed as a whole, and a list of the countries, cities, or regions covered by each series is included on the review page as well as in appendix III. The well-known and established Baedecker Guides were

not included because they are infrequently revised and are no longer distributed in the United States.

(4) ACCOMMODATION AND RESTAURANT GUIDES: Most general European guides include some accommodation listing, but guides so designated are specifically devoted to accommodations and/or restaurant suggestions.

(5) TRAIN GUIDES: These guides focus on train travel in Europe. *How to Camp Europe by Train,* reviewed in the motoring and camping chapter, is also very helpful on this subject.

(6) MOTORING AND/OR CAMPING GUIDES: This mode of travel is becoming increasingly popular, and a wide selection of guides now exists specifically for motoring and camping in Europe. Note that *Myra Waldo's Travel and Motoring Guide to Europe* is also written for the motoring traveler.

(7) BICYCLING AND/OR WALKING GUIDES: These guides cover bicycle touring in Europe and walking guides to both European cities and hiking trails. *The Youth Hosteler's Guide to Europe* is also very helpful on this subject.

Because so many accurate and up-to-date books on Europe are available, we are not including any hitchhiking guides to Europe. None of the guides available on hitchhiking in Europe has been updated since 1975, and much of the information they include is inaccurate or irrelevant. The best guide to hitchhiking in Europe, *Vagabonding in Europe and North Africa,* (New York, Random House, 1973), is no longer in print. For basic information on hitchhiking see *Let's Go: The Budget Guide to Europe.*

ANNUALLY REVISED GUIDES

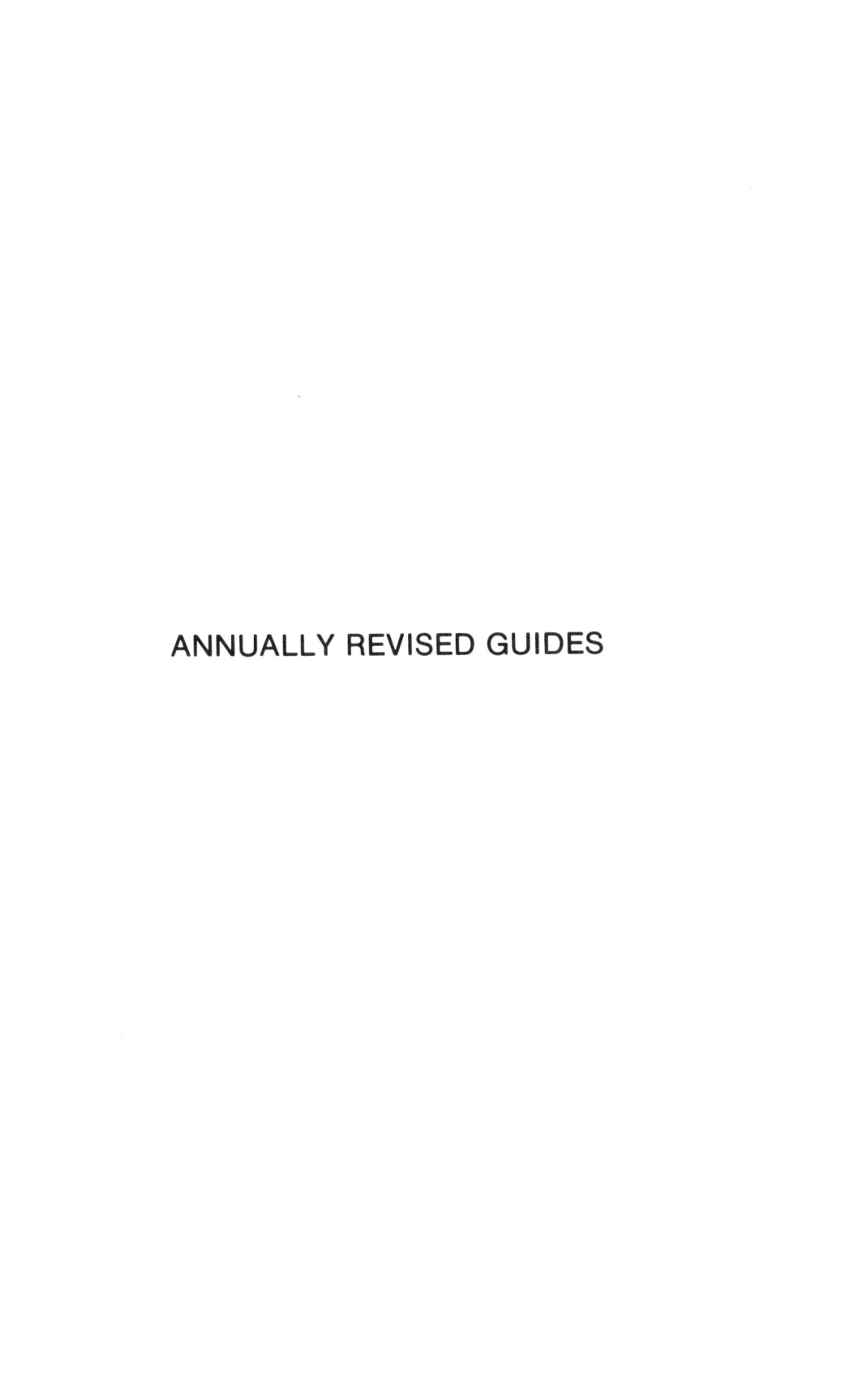

Europe on $10 a Day

Arthur Frommer
New York: Arthur Frommer, Inc.
$4.95, paperback, 691 pp., revised annually
Distributed by Simon and Schuster

Purpose and Audience

Inflation has long since forced Arthur Frommer's renknowned guide to read *Europe on $10 a Day;* nevertheless, it still provides reliable advice for the budget-minded traveler. The self-imposed budget includes meals and lodging but not transportation to or within Europe. Frommer concentrates specifically on seventeen major European cities; information on one hundred other cities and towns is condensed into one chapter of reader's suggestions.

What's included

Evaluation

For low-cost accommodations and restaurants, Frommer is hard to beat. Almost an institution, already a corporation, its one disadvantage is that many of the recommended lodgings are filled with other tourists toting *$10 a Day*. And, because it concentrates on cities, it leaves out much of the exciting, vital, and inexpensive part of the European exepriences. Another drawback is its increasingly late publication date. Whereas new editions of Fodor's Guides appear in December, as of August, 1977, the 1977-1978 edition of *Europe on $10 a Day* had just become available. Also note that information on visas and passports is *not* included.

26 EUROPE

Fielding's Low-Cost Europe

Nancy and Temple Fielding
New York: Fielding Publications
$4.95, paperback, 831 pp. revised annually

Purpose and Audience

Fielding's Low-Cost Europe is the Fielding "family's" projected forecast of the bargains and money-saving tips for travel to Europe. It contains much of the same general information and travel philosophy as the Fielding's Travel Guide to Europe but with a slant toward the inexpensive. Seventeen European countries are covered. Many cities, towns, and resorts are described briefly; and for major cities, accommodations, restaurants, nightlife spots, etc. are suggested. The book includes listings for moderate to expensive as well as budget accommodations.

What's Included

Evaluation

Fielding's Low-Cost Europe is for bargain hunters intent on seeing the Continent cheaply with a maximum of comfort. The same general drawbacks of the other Fielding publications apply here: no information on history or culture, paranoia of rackets, etc. On the other hand, full addresses and telephone numbers are included for both accommodation and restaurant listings—a big improvement over other Fielding guides. General maps of both countries and cities aid in orientation. *Fielding's Low-Cost Europe* is thus superior to *Fielding's Travel Guide to Europe* for those who desire specific information on accommodations, restaurants, and nightlife on a low to moderate budget.

Fielding's Travel Guide to Europe

Temple Fielding
New York: Fielding Publications
$9.95, paperback, 1196 pp., revised annually

Purpose and Audience

The "granddaddy" of the Fielding family publications, this guide was first conceived in partial opposition to the "deadly, tedious cathedrals and cobblestones" approach of the Baedecker and other traditional guides. It has evolved into a major guide geared to the standards of middle and affluent America. The result is an overly glib and righteous but stringent review of Europe's top accommodations, restaurants, and nightclubs. Although Fielding claims to hold to the everyday standards of middle-income Americans traveling in Europe, high to upper incomes seem necessary for the recommended style of travel. For example, $45 a day is "rock bottom" for Fielding's moderate mid-income traveler. Serious economizers are directed to *Fielding's Low-Cost Europe.*

What's Included

Evaluation

> A classic, due in part to its continued publication since 1948, Fielding's *Travel Guide to Europe* now seems a bit dated in attitude and approach. There is very little information on sights and none at all on history and culture. Remarks about natives concern themselves with attitudes toward tourists and tales of local rackets. The selective accommodation and restaurant listings lack precise addresses and prices. The Fieldings have a devoted following who can consistently gauge their reaction to the Fielding way of travel: a style that caters to American standards of comfort, is costly, and has a carefree, built-in dependence on the concierge.

Fodor's Europe

Eugene Fodor and Robert C. Fisher, Editors
New York: David McKay Company
$9.95, paperback, 751 pp., revised annually

Purpose and Audience

Fodor's Europe has more refreshing, international approach than many other generalized European guides. Directed to Canadian and Australian travelers in addition to Americans, this guide offers practical information, sight-seeing information, and accommodation and restaurant listings for thirty-four Eastern and Western European countries, as well as the USSR. Although listings range from inexpensive to deluxe, the guide is geared toward travelers with above-average means. Fodor's Europe also includes suggestions for more unusual, directed travel for those with special interests.

What's Included

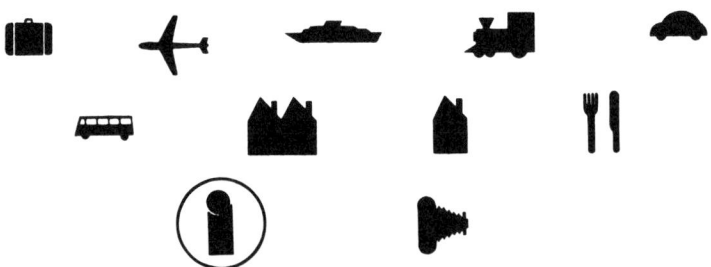

Evaluation

Whereas the Fielding guides take a "family" approach to travel writing, Fodor's receives contributions from area specialists, a fact that may make them slightly more uneven than their Fielding rival but is at the same time one of their strengths. *Fodor's* places less emphasis on accommodation and restaurant listings and instead provides more complete, comprehensive treatment of sights and transportation.

Let's Go: The Budget Guide to Europe

Harvard Student Agencies
Ralph E. Hallo, Editor
New York: E. P. Dutton and Company
$4.95, paperback, 704 pp., revised annually

Purpose and Audience

Written by students for students, *Let's Go* is chiefly concerned with inexpensive travel. Its wide coverage includes all major Western and Eastern European countries as well as Israel, Turkey, North Africa, and the USSR. It is directed toward the traveler interested in seeing and experiencing all, or as much as possible, of Europe.

What's Included

Evaluation

With budget travel its major priority, comfort and cleanliness occasionally receive short shrift in this important student guide. Errors occasionally result from multiple student authors and breadth of coverage. These disadvantages however, are usually compensated for by considerable savings. The chief advantages of *Let's Go* are its all-inclusive European coverage and its listings of rock-bottom price accommodations and student discounts. *Let's Go* emphasizes less frequently traveled areas and individual exploration and experimentation. Some indications are surfacing that *Let's Go* is resting on its laurels as the top student-and budget-oriented guide and that annual revisions are not as thorough and complete as they could be.

Myra Waldo's Travel and Motoring Guide to Europe

New York: Macmillan Publishing Company, Inc.
$9.95, paperback, 802 pp., revised annually

Purpose and Audience

Myra Waldo's Travel and Motoring Guide to Europe is somewhat of a misnomer. Several motoring routes are suggested for each of the twenty-two European countries covered, including the USSR, but directions are brief and sketchy. Special motoring tips are limited to one or two paragraphs at the end of each chapter. Hotel and restaurant suggestions are provided for capitals and only occasionally for other major cities, always without address or telephone number. This guide is geared for travelers of moderate or above budgets: prices are stiff.

What's Included

Evaluation

Myra Waldo seems most at home in Europe and employs a rambling, discursive, and, at times, repetitious style. Her approach to travel is subjective, and she is quite frank about her dislikes and likes. This guide swings between a practical accommodations and sights motoring guide and a more personal, descriptive remembrance of past trips. Organization is not consistent and information can be difficult to find. Chapters also vary on thoroughness—extremely detailed for France and super brief for Turkey. This guide is best left for tried-and-true Myra Waldo fans who enjoy her travel style.

SPECIALTY GUIDES

Fielding's Guide to Traveling with Children in Europe

Leila Hadley
New York: Fielding Publications
$9.95, hardback, 504 pp., 1974

Purpose and Audience

Fielding's Guide to Traveling with Children in Europe is filled with handy hints and practical suggestions for family travel. A substantial introduction covers all imaginable preparatory and general information. Country-by-country chapters include specifics from baby foods to a calendar of events for twenty-one European countries. Ms. Hadley postulates that travel with children need not be expensive, and she includes travel tips for all kinds of budgets.

What's Included

Evaluation

This guidebook does not attempt to be an all-encompassing, general guidebook to Europe. Ms. Hadley fills a gap in travel literature by focusing on travel from a child's point of view and emphasizing those things that can be enjoyed by both offspring and parents. It is incredibly thorough and covers a wide range of information. Well-organized and easy to use, *Fielding's*

Guide to Traveling with Children is very highly recommended for both predeparture reading and for use while traveling.

The Special Guide to Europe

John E. Whitman
New York: The New American Library, Inc.
$3.50, paperback, 284 pp., 1972

Purpose and Audience

Written especially for the first-time student traveler, *The Special Guide to Europe* has a great deal of practical information on how to save money and prevent aggravation. The author frankly opposes the "Grand Tour" approach and sets out to prescribe alternative travel possibilities. Specific hotels and restaurants are not suggested, nor are individual countries discussed. Instead, Whitman provides guidelines and necessary addresses for planning a trip to Europe on your own.

What's Included

Evaluation

For those worried about the mechanics of traveling, the wealth of pragmatic information in this book should be highly reassuring. In addition, much of the material covered here is not readily found in other guides. Direct and vivid suggestions for travel are well organized. Out-of-date price information, especially for air travel, should not deter you from consulting this book. Its commonsense approach and travel philosophy open new ways of seeing and experiencing Europe as Europeans do.

Traveler's Guide Book to Europe and Asia: Your Passport to Making it Abroad

Mark Atlas
New York: Robert Speller & Sons, Publishers, Inc.
$2.95, paperback, 249 pp., 1973

Purpose and Audience

A *Traveler's Guide Book to Europe and Asia* is your passport for making it abroad. Based partially on the author's own global experiences, the first half of the guide is devoted to general information and travel philosophy. The second half is a compilation of vital statistics covering visas, health, money, etc., for over sixty cities and countries. Although Atlas claims to address tourists and travelers alike (there is a difference), the book will appeal more to the latter, specifically those on rock-bottom to moderate budgets. This is *not* a guide to specific accommodations, restaurants, and transportation. Instead, it is a handbook of information necessary for travel in Europe and Asia.

What's Included

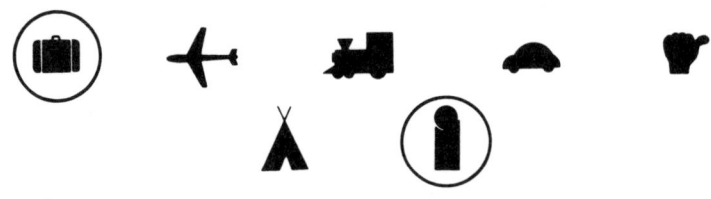

Evaluation

This lesser-known guide is a real find. It supplies valuable, practical, and level-headed advice on topics most guidebooks usually ignore: chapters range from pretravel checklists to how to handle beggars. Although the 1973 publication date renders most listed prices and visa regulations obsolete, the general information provided more than makes up for any discrepancies. Lack of an index complicates matters some. In spite of the above disadvantages, the *Traveler's Guide Book* is far above and beyond most other rock-bottom-oriented guidebooks. Including both Asia and Europe under one cover, *Traveler's Guide Book* will serve an increasing audience as the more traditional travel boundaries continue to expand.

The Traveller's Survival Kit: Europe

Roger Brown
Oxford, England: Vacation-Work
$3.95, paperback, 159 pp., revised annually
Distributed by Gaylord Professional Publications
Syracuse, New York 13221

Purpose and Audience

Written for British travelers to the Continent, *The Traveller's Survival Kit* will also suit the needs of Canadians and Americans traveling in Europe. This is a guide to the "nuts and bolts" of European travel; advice ranges from police attitudes to different types of possible accommodations. Specific hotel and restaurant suggestions are not given; instead, instructions on how to manage on your own are provided. Information covering eighteen European countries applies to both novice and experienced traveler.

What's Included

Evaluation

The Traveller's Survival Kit provides a wealth of information designed for far more than mere survival in Europe. Much of the information will clue you in to tips and events that only natives know. Essential addresses and telephone numbers for emergencies are provided. A calendar of events for each country listing holidays and festivals is an added plus. This small volume will make a great supplement to a guidebook to hotels and sights and is recommended reading for pretravel planning as well as for use once on the road.

Whitman's Off Season Travel Guide to Europe

John Whitman
New York: St. Martin's Press
$6.95, paperback, 692 pp., 1976

Purpose and Audience

Whitman's Off Season Travel Guide claims to introduce travelers to "Europe at its best from September to May." The twenty-five individual country chapters are divided regionally, with information on towns, weather, hotels, and restaurants. Some travel experience is assumed; minimal information on preparation and transportation to Europe is provided. Although off season travel usually implies bargain or inexpensive rates, the majority of the accommodation and restaurant listings cater to the rich or well-off.

What's Included

Evaluation

Unfortunately, this book does not live up to its potential as an off season European travel guide. Perhaps one problem is that Whitman attempts to cover too much of Europe. The result is a quick, once-over approach that forecloses in-depth treatment of the advantages and disadvantages of off season travel. Information is sometimes incomplete and thus misleading. One good feature is a chapter on ski resorts in Europe. Even that, however, could be expanded.

Youth Hosteler's Guide to Europe

Youth Hostel Association
New York: Macmillan Publishing Co., Inc.
$3.95, paperback, 494 pp., 1977

Purpose and Audience

The *Youth Hosteler's Guide to Europe* is the intended companion to the *International Youth Hostel Handbook, volume I,* which lists vital information, addresses, and prices for youth hostels in Europe. The *Youth Hosteler's Guide* provides basic travel information and itineraries geared to hostelers traveling by foot or bicycle. Advice on basic preparation and transportation to Europe is left to other guides, but facts on flora, fauna, history, literature, and art are provided for the twenty-one European countries covered.

What's Included

Evaluation

This guide succeeds in achieving the Youth Hostel Association's aim of getting beyond traditional "sightseeing." It is a culturally sensitive, broad survey introduction to the countries and peoples of Europe. Although it is specifically directed to hostelers, the touring routes may be of interest to motorists and train travelers who wish to explore beyond the well-worn, heavily trafficked tourist routes. Combine it with its companion volume, the *International Youth Hostel Handbook,* and you have all the basic information for a hostel adventure or off-the-beaten-track travel in Europe.

SERIES GUIDES ABOUT SPECIFIC COUNTRIES, CITIES, OR REGIONS

A to Z World Travel Guides

Robert S. Kane
Garden City, New York: Doubleday & Company
$6.95 to $9.95, all hardback, issued periodically

Purpose and Audience

Robert Kane, prolific writer and veteran traveler, has written this series. Dating from the 1963 *Asia A to Z* to the most recent guide, the 1977 *Italy A to Z: A Grand Tour of the Classic Cities,* the series comprises guides to destinations around the world. Kane conveys a selective and highly personal view of a "compendium of requisite destinations," which includes sights as well as evaluations of "creature comforts," i.e., hotels, restaurants, etc. He addresses travelers with budgets ranging from moderate to luxurious. The latest guides in the series tend to place an emphasis on cities.

What's Included

Evaluation

Although the guides vary in organization and emphasis, Kane's particular style appears to be the evocation of travel in the manner of the "18th Century Grand Tour of the Continent" (note especially *Grand Tour A to Z: The Capitals of Europe*). The advantages of Kane's A to Z guides are similar to those of Myra Waldo's travel guides; their personal and subjective style allows the reader consistently to gauge the author's opinion on a large number of areas. Kane, unlike Myra Waldo, introduces an increasingly popular notion: the idea of travel with a theme, which perhaps renders his guides more successful.

Books Included in This Series

Africa A to Z
Asia A to Z
Eastern Europe A to Z
Grand Tour A to Z: The Capitals of Europe
Italy A to Z: A Grand Tour of the Classic Cities
London A to Z
Paris A to Z

Arthur Frommer's Guides

New York: The Frommer/Pasmantier Publishing Corporation
$1.95, all paperback, revised periodically
Distributed by Simon and Schuster

Purpose and Audience

The Arthur Frommer's Guides to cities promise hotels, restaurants, and tours at prices ranging from "truly low-budget to luxury, with a generous sampling of prices in between." As with the other Frommer Guides, the emphasis is on accommodations and restaurants. Information on transportation to the city or on visas and passports is *not* included.

What's Included

Evaluation

Concerned with the present and those aspects of the cities that attract tourists, the Arthur Frommer's Guides adequately cover the practical aspects of what to do, see, eat, and buy and where to stay. Additional information is provided for day-trip excursions and other principal sights and attractions. Frommer fans will profit from these handy, pocket-sized guides for longer sojourns in a specific city.

Books Included in This Series

Arthur Frommer's Guide to
    Athens
    Ireland/Dublin/Shannon
    Lisbon/Madrid/Costa del Sol
    London
    Paris
    Rome

48 EUROPE

Berlitz Travel Guides

Lausanne, Switzerland: Editions Berlitz, S.A.
all $2.95, all paperback, revised periodically
Distributed by Macmillan Publishing Company, Inc.,
866 Third Avenue, New York, New York 10022

Purpose and Audience

Berlitz, of language fame, now publishes this series of guides to tourist-frequented areas and cities. Directed toward the jet traveler, they concentrate on compact and colorful presentations. Brief histories of areas or cities are followed by "What to See" and "Day Excursions." Practical information is color coded and entered alphabetically in the back. Regional specialties are described, but no specific restaurants or hotels are suggested.

What's Included

Evaluation

Capitalizing on the compact format, the Berlitz Travel Guides present the standard, tourist-oriented jargon backed by glossy photographs. Small and slim enough to fit into your back pocket, the information contained within is necessarily brief. The Berlitz Guides will direct you to major sights, but not much more.

Books Included in This Series

Amsterdam
Athens

Canary Islands
Corfu
Costa Brava
Costa del Sol and Andalusia
Costa Dorada and Barcelona
Crete
Dubrovnik and Southern Dalmatia
Florence
Ibiza and Formentera
Istria and Croatian Coast
Leningrad
Loire Valley
London
Madeira
Madrid
Majorca and Minorca
Moscow
Rhodes
Rome and the Vatican
Split and Dalmatia
Venice

50 EUROPE

Blue Guides

London: Ernest Benn Limited
$5.95 to $17.95, hardback and paperback, revised periodically
Distributed by Rand McNally & Company, P.O. Box 7600
Chicago, Illinois 60680

Purpose and Audience

The Blue Guides, well known and respected throughout Europe, are guidebooks in the traditional sense. Extensive background information for each region, city, and sight provides more than enough material from which to choose whatever suits your needs. Broad coverage of a wide range of sights and accommodations should appeal to travelers of all budgets. Blue Guides are perhaps best appreciated by those who want to see more than the regular tourist-oriented spots.

What's Included

Evaluation

The Blue Guides attempt to guide and inform prospective travelers, not to cajole or create an artificial enthusiasm. The emphasis is on correct information; the guide seeks to stimulate rather than to sell. Comparison with the Nagel's Encyclopedia-Guides reveals the Blue Guides as somewhat more historically and artistically oriented and generally more complete. The practical information, in addition, is integrated into the text. The Blue Guides succeed in their goal to provide a wealth of information for the serious traveler.

Books Included in This Series

The Adriatic Coast
Athens and Environs
Belgium and Luxembourg
Bernese Oberland
Crete
Denmark
England
Greece
Holland
Ireland
London
Lucerne
Malta
Northern Italy
Northwestern France
Paris
Rome and Environs
Scotland
South of France
Southern Italy
Southern Spain
Wales
Yugoslavia

Dollar Wise Guides

New York: The Frommer/Pasmantier Publishing Co.
$3.95 to $4.50, all paperback, revised periodically
Distributed by Simon and Schuster

Purpose and Audience

These guidebooks give specific, practical suggestions for hotels and restaurants, sight-seeing attractions, and nightlife in the major cities and towns of five European countries. They enhance the appeal of budget travel, revealing that it is not always necessary to pay "scalper's prices" to enjoy a country's charms, comforts, and foods. Although the audience is defined as travelers of all budgets, from rock bottom to carefree, the book will appeal most to travelers on moderate and above budgets.

What's Included

Evaluation

The Dollar Wise Guides delve a little more deeply into the outer provinces and regions of a country than the more traditional and more general *Europe on $10 a Day*. The inclusion of "deluxe" hotels and restaurants and the concentration on "moderate" budgets distinguish the Dollar Wise Guides from the *$10 a Day* country series. One feature shared by both is a section plugging a "sponsor airline," which may bias the transportation section. Again, like the other Frommer Guides, the forte of the Dollar Wise Guides is hotel and restaurant suggestions.

Books Included in This Series

Dollar Wise Guide to
    England
    France
    Germany
    Italy
    Portugal

Fodor's Guides

Eugene Fodor and Robert C. Fisher, Editors
New York: David McKay Company
$2.95 to $14.95, paper and hardback, revised periodically

Purpose and Audience

Unlike Frommer's Guides, Fodor's Guides to countries and cities focus on sights, culture, and history rather than on accommodations and restaurants. A guidebook in the more traditional sense, Fodor's addresses travelers of all budgets but is more relevant to cost-wise moderate budget or above travelers.

54 EUROPE

What's Included

Evaluation

> These guides are well organized and thorough, presenting many interesting travel options and facts. They are well worth their price as a supplement to the rock bottom, student-oriented guides. Their strength is in their combination of practical and background information. The detailed comprehensive coverage is particularly useful to travelers who plan to stay for an extensive visit. Accommodation and restaurant suggestions are plentiful, but descriptions are brief.

Books Included in This Series

> Fodor's
>> Australia, New Zealand, and the South Pacific
>> Austria
>> Belgium and Luxembourg
>> Carribean, Bahamas, and Bermuda
>> Cruises Everywhere
>> Czecholslovakia
>> Egypt
>> Europe
>> Europe on a Budget
>> Europe Talking
>> France
>> Germany
>> Great Britain
>> Greece
>> Holland
>> Hungary

India
Iran
Ireland
Israel
Italy
Japan and Korea
London
Mexico
Morocco
Paris
Peking
Portugal
Railways of the World
Scandinavia
South America
Southeast Asia
Soviet Union
Spain
Switzerland
Tunisia
Turkey
Venice
Vienna
Yugoslavia

The Holiday Travel Guides

New York: Random House
all $2.95, all paperback, revised periodically

Purpose and Audience

The Holiday Guides offer commonsense information for selected countries and major cities of Europe and Mexico. The guides include the usual gamut of travel information, ranging from preparation and historical background to limited sections on transportation, hotels, and accommodations. The intended audience is large; much of the information will apply to moderate and budget travelers. Rock bottom or low-budget tips are not included.

What's Included

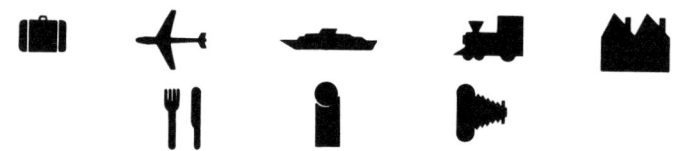

Evaluation

These guides to cities and countries provide more specific information than can be found in a general guide to Europe. Informative sections on historical and cultural background, supplemented with black and white photographs, will orient the novice and aid in itinerary planning. A good, standard, tourist-oriented guide.

Books Included in This Series

Britain
The Caribbean and the Bahamas

France
Greece and the Aegean Islands
Ireland
Israel
Italy
London
Mexico
Paris
Rome
Scandinavia
Spain
West Germany

Michelin Green Guide* (English Editions)

Paris, France: Michelin Company
all $4.95, all paperback, revised periodically
Distributed by Michelin Guides and Maps, P.O. Box 188,
Roslyn Heights, New York 11577

Purpose and Audience

The Michelin Guides, published by the tire company of the same name, were among the first travel guides written primarily for the motorist. Since then, Michelin Green Guides, translated from French, have earned a well-deserved reputation for providing thorough and intelligent discussions of the history, art, architecture, and sights of an area. The guides for countries and

*Michelin Red Guides are reviewed in the accommodations chapter.

58   EUROPE

areas include maps, suggested itineraries, and tours, as well as introductory and practical information. More specific information and Michelin-rated sights and cities are covered alphabetically.

What's Included

Evaluation

Michelin Guides provide interesting historical and cultural background for traverlers interested in in-depth coverage of an area, coverage that does not neglect to provide a broad overview as well. They are lightweight and slim, thus making them excellent on-site companions to a more general guidebook. Michelin Green Guides are very highly recommended for pre-travel planning and are useful on the road.

Books Included in This Series

Austria
Brittany
Chateaux of the Loire
Dordogna
French Riviera
Germany
Italy
Normandy
Paris
Portugal
Spain
Switzerland

Nagel's Encyclopedia-Guides

Geneva, Switzerland: Nagel Publishers
$4.00 to $35, hardcover and paperback, revised periodically
Distributed by Hippocrene Books, Inc., 171 Madison Avenue, New York, New York 10016

Purpose and Audience

The Nagel's Encyclopedia-Guides cater to the inquisitive and independent traveler. The geographic, economic, and demographic features of towns, regions, and countries occupy top rank beside the traditional historic and artistic information. Practical information is gathered into one chapter at the end of the book.

What's Included

Evaluation

Updated versions of this time-honored series, the new Nagel's Encyclopedia-Guides provide in-depth information for veteran globe trotter and first-time traveler alike. Compared to the Blue Guides, the information is more general and less historically oriented. The choice between Nagel's Encyclopedia-Guides or Blue Guides will be a matter of personal preference, based perhaps on their differing organization.

EUROPE

Books Included in This Series

Algeria
Austria
Balearic Islands
Bulgaria
Ceylon
Chateaux of the Loire
China
Cyprus
Czechoslovakia
Denmark-Greenland
Egypt
Finland
French and Italian Riviera
Germany (Federal Republic)
Great Britain and Ireland
Greece
Gulf Emirates
Holland
Hungary
Iceland
India and Nepal
Iran
Israel
Italy
Japan
Leningrad and Its Environs
Malta
Mexico
Morocco
Moscow and Its Environs
Poland
Portugal (Madeira, the Azores)
Rome
Rumania
Spain
Sweden
Thailand, Angkor (Cambodia)

Turkey
USSR
Yugoslavia

Sunset Travel Guides

Menlo Park, California: Lane Publishing Company
$2.95 to $3.95, all paperback, revised periodically

Purpose and Audience

The editors of the successful West Coast magazine, *Sunset*, also offer a series of international travel guides. Not "guidebooks" in the strictest sense, the Sunset Guides provide interesting, thoroughly researched background information on the areas covered. Although hotel and restaurant suggestions are sometimes included, these guides are best used as a general introduction to the travel destination.

What's Included

Evaluation

The Sunset Guides make enjoyable prevoyage reading for serious and armchair travelers alike. Emphasis is placed on cultural considerations. The plentiful photographs and highlighted interest sections will aid in planning travel itineraries, but the large format makes it difficult to take the books along.

Books Included in This Series

Australia
Europe: Discovery Trips
Islands of the South Pacific
Japan
Mexico
New Zealand
The Orient
Southeast Asia

$10-A-Day Guides

Arthur Frommer
New York: Arthur Frommer, Inc.
$3.95 to $4.95, all paperback, revised periodically
Distributed by Simon and Schuster

Purpose and Audience

Offspring of the very successful *Europe on $10 a Day*, the $5-, $10-, $15-A-Day Guides for individual countries and cities have a similar underlying goal: to suggest hotels and restaurants where travelers can "live simply, inexpensively, and yet in surprising comfort." The basic format of the two series is the same, although the authors differ. The figures in titles indicate travel budget for accommodation and meals; transportation and entertainment are extra.

What's Included

Evaluation

The goal of this series is to provide a handy collection of budget restaurants and accommodations. Like the other Frommer Guides, the $10-A-Day series specifically concentrates on the practical aspects of where to eat and sleep and are very brief on what to see. Travelers interested in historical and cultural information should supplement them with other guides.

Books Included in This Series

England on $15 a Day
Europe on $10 a Day
Greece on $10 a Day
India (plus Sri Lanka and Nepal) on $5 & $10 a Day
Ireland on $10 a Day
Israel on $10 & $15 a Day
Mexico and Guatemala on $10 a Day
New Zealand on $10 a Day
Scandinavia on $15 & $20 a Day
South America on $10 & 15 a Day
Spain and Morocco (plus the Canary Islands) on $10 & $15 a Day
Turkey on $5 & $10 a Day

ACCOMMODATION AND RESTAURANT GUIDES

AA Budget Guide to Europe

Hampshire, England: Automobile Association
$6.95, paperback, 236 pp., revised annually
Distributed by Standing Orders, Inc., 156 Fifth Avenue,
New York, New York 10010

Purpose and Audience

The *AA Budget Guide to Europe* lists over five-thousand low-cost places to stay in twelve continental European countries. Published by Great Britain's Automobile Association, the guide also contains helpful preparatory information and motoring tips. Cities and towns are listed alphabetically within country sections. Also included is a handy forty-two page atlas and, for this year's edition, a section on the vineyards of Bordeaux.

What's Included

Evaluation

This is a practical and handy guide to not only AA recommended low-cost hotels but also motels, farm houses, and pensions. In addition, a section on accommodations for rent adds to the low-cost European vacation possibilities. Completeness of listings varies from country to country, and captial cities are especially weak. These drawbacks are reduced if the guide is used along with a guide oriented to major cities. Another drawback is that the practical information is directed to British regulations and standards; again, a drawback that is not too difficult to overcome.

AAA European Accommodations

American Automobile Association
Falls Church, Virginia: American Automobile Association
$5.00, paperback, 407 pp., revised biennially
Distribution policies determined by individual AAA clubs. For more information contact the nearest AAA office or write to AAA, 8111 Gatehouse Road, Falls Church, Virginia 22042

Purpose and Audience

Published by the AAA as a service for its members, *AAA European Accommodations* is the intended companion volume to the *AAA Travel Guide to Europe*. This compilation of accommodations and restaurants is geared to motorists of moderate incomes. Its hotel and restaurant listings include essential information, brief descriptions, and the AAA stamp of approval. Organization is alphabetical by country and city. *AAA European Accommodations* is often available free for members.

What's Included

Evaluation

This directory lists restaurants and accommodations for many of the small towns of Europe—very helpful for the motoring tourist. Its alphabetical arrangement, however, is only useful after an itinerary has been drafted. A very reliable guide based on strict AAA standards.

Castle Hotels of Europe

Robert P. Long
East Meadow, New York: Robert P. Long
$4.95, paperback, 180 pp., 1977
Distributed by Hastings House, Publisher, Inc.

Purpose and Audience

This recently revised and updated guide of castle hotels includes listings for nineteen Western European countries. Each listing includes the castle's name, address, and a brief description. The hotels are also categorized according to rates; and although most castle hotels are over $25 per day per person, a surprising number are under $15 per day per person. Some castle restaurants are also included.

What's Included

Evaluation

This guide will be of interest to those who want to explore the ancient abbeys and accessible castle homes of Western Europe. The descriptions are brief but adequate, and maps with locations of the castle hotels facilitate planning.

Country Inns and Back Roads, European Edition

Norman T. Simpson
Stockbridge, Massachusetts: Berkshire Traveler Press
$4.95, paperback, 344 pp., 1976

Purpose and Audience

Country Inns and Back Roads, European Edition offers an alternative European experience to the capital city, whirlwind tour. The author, Norman T. Simpson, explores a selection of inns and guesthouses in nine European countries, including Scandinavia, the Netherlands, the United Kingdom, Austria, and Spain. Each inn and country house is amply described, with a sprinkling of personal anecdotes for additional flavor. Budget concerns are not of primary importance; prices range from moderate to expensive.

What's Included

Evaluation

This is a guide with a very specific purpose: only a special kind of accommodation and a few restaurants are discussed. The Berkshire Traveler philosophy of back road adventures and native charm should appeal to both experienced and novice European travelers. Mr. Simpson employs a chatty style that may appear naive to some. *Country Inns* provides enjoyable pretravel reading, and the guide should prove useful for those looking for accommodations while traveling the back roads.

Fielding's Selected Favorites: Hotels and Inns, Europe

Dodge Temple Fielding
New York: Fielding Publications
$4.95, paperback, 494 pp., revised annually

Purpose and Audience

Fielding's Selected Favorites is an accommodation guide to some of Europe's most exclusive hotels and inns. Written by Dodge Temple Fielding, son of the reknowned Fieldings, it ranks some three hundred hotels as "Fielding's favorites" and an additional five hundred as "alternates."

What's Included

Evaluation

Although the guide purports to address a wide range of travel budgets, most hotels listed are in the $50 per double/per night range or above. The addresses of some of the hotels and listings of their amenities are indicated in tables in the back, but addresses for the alternatives are sometimes difficult to find or nonexistent. Definitely a guide for those with well-padded wallets and a passion for luxury.

International Youth Hostel Handbook: Volume I, Europe and Mediterranean Countries*

Herts, England: International Youth Hostel Federation
$3.25, paperback, 160 pp., revised annually
Distributed by American Youth Hostel Offices across the country and by American Youth Hostels, Inc., National Campus, Delaplane, Virginia 22025

Purpose and Audience

The International Youth Hostel Association provides simple, inexpensive lodgings for members. This handbook lists all youth hostels alphabetically by country. Specifics on costs, sizes, and facilities are given in three languages, and telephone numbers are provided. Also included is information on how to obtain a Youth Hostel membership card and how to book accommodations in advance.

What's Included

Evaluation

The information is concise, complete, and, once the symbols are mastered, easy to understand. Included is a map that graphically illustrates hostel locations and major routes. For hostelers, this pocket-sized guide is invaluable.

*Volume II of the International Youth Hostel Handbook is also available. It contains a listing of hostels in Africa, America, Asia, and Australia.

Michelin Red Guides*

Paris, France: Michelin Co.
$7.95 to $9.95, hardback, revised annually
Distributed by Michelin Guides and Maps, P.O. Box 188,
Roslyn Heights, New York 11577

Purpose and Audience

These annually revised, multilingual Red Guides are intended as companion volumes to the Michelin Green Guides series. Also aimed at motorists, the Red Guides offer a rated selection of hotels and restaurants. A wide range of information is presented through symbols. The Red Guides also provide information such as years of the best local wines and addresses of reputable garages.

What's Included

Evaluation

A Michelin star of approval usually guarantees excellent fare and lodging. In fact, the Michelin guides transcend the needs of a travel-oriented audience... many use the Red Guides as permanent directories to restaurants and lodgings. The Michelin Red Guides are very highly recommended. Through the wide range of accommodations and restaurants presented, they serve budget traveler and big spender alike.

*Michelin Green Guides (English Editions) are reviewed in the chapter on series guides to European countries, cities, and regions.

Books Included in This Series

>Benelux
>Camping in France
>France
>Germany
>Great Britain and Ireland
>Italy
>London
>Paris-English
>Paris-French
>Spain and Portugal

Student Hostels and Tour Activities: Handbook for the Young Traveler

International Student Travel Conference and Swiss Student Travel Office
Zurich, Switzerland: Swiss Student Travel Office
$1.00, paperback, 120 pp., revised annually
Distributed by Council on International Educational Exchange, 777 United Nations Plaza, New York, New York 10017

Purpose and Audience

>Like youth hostels, student hostels and hotels provide lodgings for young people. While they do not require membership, as do youth hostels, international student I.D. cards are frequently required. This booklet lists all

the essential information for these hostels, including amenities and prices. In addition, information on student tours and flights is provided along with the addresses of International Student Travel Conference-affiliated offices.

What's Included

Evaluation

Hotels and hostels are listed alphabetically for thirty-seven countries around the world, but the majority of listings concentrate on European countries. The selection varies greatly from country to country, but even where the number of suggestions is slim, it can lead the student traveler to low-cost accommodations. For the price of one dollar, this booklet will easily compensate for its initial cost. A very handy booklet.

TRAIN GUIDES

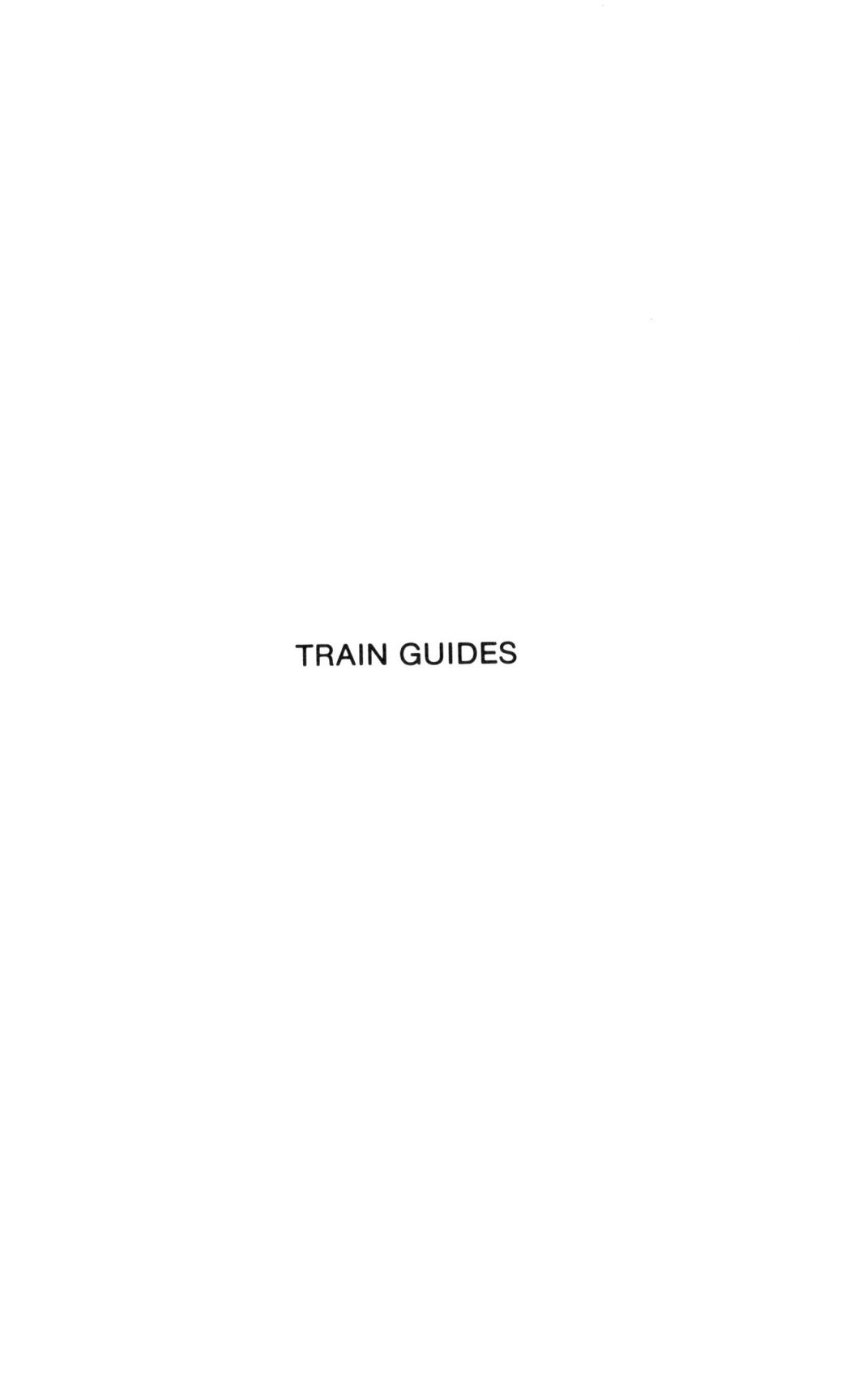

Baxter's Eurailpass Travel Guide

Robert Baxter
Alexandria, Virginia: Rail-Europe
$7.95, paperback, 503 pp., revised annually

Purpose and Audience

Baxter's Eurailpass Travel Guide is an attempt to compress into one guide all the essential information for Eurailpass train travel through thirteen European countries. The guide thus includes orientation maps indicating hotels located near railroad stations, sightseeing excursions and walking tours for major cities, information on public transportation between stations, and much more. Although Eurailpass travel can be economical, Baxter's Eurailpass Travel Guide is not directed toward the rock bottom traveler. The prices are geared to moderate-budget travelers.

What's Included

Evaluation

Underwritten in part by Icelandic Airlines, the guide contains a substantial section devoted to Icelandic fares and tours in both Iceland and Luxembourg. The travel philosophy tends toward "Grand Tour" whirlwind traveling, with no more than two days spent in even major cities. Baxter's Eurailpass Travel Guide manages to pack in a great deal of general information concerning train travel in specific countries. The encyclopedic, "all-purpose-guide" approach necessarily dilutes some of the material. To be recommended are sections on areas outside the main cities and on walking tours. Good for pretravel reading and orientation; useful for the quick train travel tour of Europe.

Enjoy Europe by Train

William J. Dunn
New York: Charles Scribner's Sons
$4.95, paperback, 255 pp., 1974

Purpose and Audience

Enjoy Europe by Train is a sensible guide to train travel in Europe. A general introduction to the advantages of traveling by train is followed by a separate chapter on special fares, baggage, and scenic routes for sixteen major Western European countries. The book is aimed at travelers of all incomes; the Eurailpass and student railpass are discussed but are *not* the focus of the book. Appendixes cover U.S. passport requirements, timetables, symbols, temperature conversion charts, etc.

What's Included

Evaluation

Dunn's chatty description of European highlights provides a nice introduction for travelers planning their first itinerary. Likewise, the train travel information will aid experienced travelers. One drawback is that this guide has not been revised since 1974. For more up-to-date and specific information on the intricacies of European railways, consult the *Eurail Guide* or *Baxter's Eurailpass Travel Guide.*

Eurail Guide: How to Travel Europe by Train

Marvin L. Saltzman and Kathryn Saltzman Muileman
Malibu, California: The Saltzman Companies
$5.95, paperback, 430 pp., revised annually

Purpose and Audience

The Saltzman family publishes this guide annually for inexperienced and experienced travelers alike. All aspects of train travel, from Eurailpasses to the Trans-Siberian express, are handled in this small but thick pocketbook guide. *Not* a guide to specific countries or hotels, the Saltzman father-daughter team concentrates on teaching you how to manage on your own traveling by train.

82   EUROPE

What's Included

Evaluation

This informative guide should be of special interest to the neophyte traveler who is going to cover a lot of territory by train. The Saltzman book includes detailed, tested itineraries, approximate train fares and schedules, and a chapter on whether to buy a Eurail pass. Especially helpful are the chapter on common rail travel questions in four languages and the chapter covering rail service data and itineraries for forty-four non-European countries. Experienced independent travelers might want to skim this guide before taking off; more inexperienced travelers might read it carefully and take it along in addition to a sights-accommodations guide.

Europe by Eurail

George Wright Ferguson
Columbus, Ohio: George Wright Ferguson
$6.00, paperback, 406 pp., revised annually

Purpose and Audience

Europe by Eurail promotes a "base city-day excursion" method of travel through Europe whereby travelers establish a "base" in a city from which to make numerous day excursions, always returning to the same hotel. Coupled with the Eurailpass, this method of travel is unharried and relaxed, as well as inexpensive—or so the author says. *Europe by Eurail* is a guide to this specific mode of travel; it covers twelve major "base" cities in Europe and various day excursions from them, replete with instructions, sights, and schedules. Hotel and restaurant suggestions are left to other guides. *Europe by Eurail* is oriented towards experienced and inexperienced travelers alike.

What's Included

Evaluation

Europe by Eurail presents a viable, interesting mode of European travel. Its guidelines are flexible enough to allow independence, exploration, and change; but the tours themselves take in only the most obvious, principal sights. More in-depth information for cities will be necessary for the type of travel suggested by the author. All in all, *Europe by Eurail* makes for good pre-travel reading for train travelers and would be useful once traveling. Its format, however, necessitates its use in conjunction with other guidebooks.

MOTORING AND CAMPING GUIDES

AA Guide to Camping and Caravaning on the Continent

Hampshire, England: The Automobile Association
$8.95, paperback, 368 pp., revised annually
Distributed by Standing Orders, Inc., P.O. Box 183, Patterson, New York 12563

Purpose and Audience

The *AA Guide to Camping and Caravaning on the Continent* is more than just a directory to campsites. Introductory remarks include weather and electrical information and the rundown on fuels, insurance, and mountain passes. Written for British Automobile Association members, this compact guide should serve all campers. Nearly five thousand campsites are organized alphabetically by town or city for eighteen European countries. In addition, brief sections of practical information on history, major cities, and camping conditions precede each country section. A seventy-three-page atlas indicates campsite locations.

What's Included

Evaluation

The *AA Guide to Camping* manages to squeeze comprehensive listings into a relatively small format. Added welcome features are the brief descriptions and comments about AA-inspected sites, which are provided in addition to the standard AA symbols. It is well organized and easy to use. The *AA Guide to Camping* is recommended for campers and caravaners who want more information than just a listing of campsites.

EUROPE

AA Guide to Continental Motoring

Hampshire, England: The Automobile Association
$6.95, paperback, 556 pp., revised annually
Distributed by Standing Orders, Inc., P.O. Box 183, Patterson, New York 12563

Purpose and Audience

A British Automobile Association publication, the *AA Guide to Continental Motoring* lists more than nine thousand AA-approved hotels and garages in twenty-one countries. A travel and motoring guide combined, the specific country chapters are preceded by a lengthy introduction on preparation for a motoring holiday.

What's Included

Evaluation

The directory to reputable garages on the Continent is very helpful and apparently a rare commodity in a motoring guide. Additional special features are a motoring tour of a historic battlefield of West Belgium and a review of the ferry services operated between Great Britain and the Continent. Careful attention to detail and thorough preparation will aid experienced motorists and neophytes alike. Its maps, however, are more general than the Hallwag *Europa Touring*.

AAA Travel Guide to Europe

American Autombile Association
Falls Church, Virginia: The American Automobile Association
$5.00, paperback, 576 pp., 1977
Distribution policies determined by individual AAA clubs. For more information, contact the nearest AAA office or write to AAA, 8111 Gatehouse Road, Falls Church, Virginia 22042

Purpose and Audience

The *AAA Travel Guide to Europe* is billed as a "catalog of travel information." The American Automobile Association publishes this guide along with a companion volume, *European Accommodations*, as a service to members. Although the guide primarily addresses motorists, it may be of interest to other travelers as well. A general section on travel preparation precedes individual chapters on thirty-five Eastern and Western European countries, including the USSR. Chapters consist of general tourist information and an alphabetical listing and description of towns, cities, and major sights.

What's Included

Evaluation

The guide aims at survey coverage of the principal European tourist attractions. The information provided is of necessity general but does manage to touch on the essential facts of history, culture, etc. In addition to standard travel advice, the guide includes helpful orientation maps and brief, informative subchapters on capital cities. The guide's atlaslike organization will be of special interest to motorists intent on traveling long distances.

Enjoy Europe by Car

William J. Dunn
New York: Charles Scribner's Sons
$5.95, paperback, 303 pp., 1976

Purpose and Audience

Enjoy Europe by Car is not a guide to specific routes, places, accommodations, or restaurants. Its goal is to show American tourists "how to travel in Europe as the Europeans do" and "how to make your own decisions." The first third of *Enjoy Europe* is devoted to general preparation and practical information concerning motoring in Europe. The remaining two-thirds consists of introductory chapters on twenty-two Western and Southern European countries. A series of appendixes packs a good deal of practical information, charts, and conversion tables into a concise format.

What's Included

Evaluation

Dunn sets out to cover everything you need to know about driving abroad. He succeeds fairly well: the book is crammed with useful information and tips based on personal experience. At times he attempts to be over-thorough and ends up sounding a bit stodgy. And the sometimes random and rambling organization can make information difficult to locate. *Enjoy Europe* will be most appreciated by the novice traveler who prefers to be well informed. This guide's greatest asset is as pretravel reading for motorists. Although useful, the appendixes do not justify taking the whole book on the road.

Europa Camping and Caravaning

H. Dieter Schmol
Stuttgart, Germany: Drei Brunnen Verlag
$6.50, paperback, 796 pp., revised annually
Distributed by Europa Camping and Caravaning,
2306 Sixth Street, Clay Center, Kansas 67432

Purpose and Audience

The multilingual directory covers not only Europe but North Africa and the Middle East. *Europa Camping* and Caravaning staff members personally check out campsites for comfort and facilities before including the listing. The sites are grouped by region for each country.

What's Included

Evaluation

The elaborate campsite coding system and triptique guide alphabetization is confusing at first. Maps are interspersed with just enough information roughly to locate the campsite; more detailed road maps will be necessary for travel. Like the *Rand McNally European Campground Guide,* this guide is just a directory of campsites, but all have been personally checked out by the *Europa Camping and Caravaning* staff. The listings are very complete and so detailed as to indicate the water temperature of lakes and oceans. An additional bonus is a discount for *Europa Camping and Caravaning* owners at some five hundred European campsites.

Europa Touring: Motoring Guide of Europe

Bern, Switzerland: Hallwag Verlag
$20.95, hardback, 796 pp., revised annually
Distributed by American Map Company, 1926 Broadway,
New York, New York 10023

Purpose and Audience

This multilingual "bible" of motoring in Europe is published by the prestigious map company, Hallwag. Country and city maps are followed by international motoring tips. More specific motoring information is included in separate country sections in addition to general information on history, geography, sports, etc. *Europa Touring* highlights and follows information on each area with an alphabetical directory of towns and lists of hotel accommodations. This Hallwag guide is directed to the international motorist of moderate to deluxe budget and covers thirty Western and Eastern European countries. No travel preparation material is included.

What's Included

Evaluation

The detailed maps and motoring instructions provided by *Europa Touring* would be essential to any motorist. Although pages are color coded, the organization and key to symbols is fairly complex. In addition, the rating system for hotels and sights is not explained. Despite these organizational problems, *Europa Touring* contains a vast amount of information in a relatively compact format and as an atlas is difficult to beat.

European Camping and Caravaning

Bob and Claudette Cope
New York: Drake Publishers, Inc.
$4.95, paperback, 258 pp., 1974

Purpose and Audience

European Camping and Caravaning explains "how to" for European-style camping trips. The audience ranges from primitive backpackers to opulent campers in mobile homes. Strategies for planning open the book, followed by a rundown of the various eschelons of motor camping and a listing of selected favorite campsites. This is not a guide in the traditional sense; the major emphasis of the book is to introduce you to the possibilities and low-cost practicalities of European camping as the Europeans do it.

What's Included

Evaluation

The Copes tackle all aspects of camping and caravaning in Europe without becoming bogged down in sundry details. They provide an excellent introduction to camping; and their facts, combined with their personal experiences, make for pleasurable reading. The 1974 publication date renders most prices obsolete, but the wealth of information more than makes up for any inconveniences this might cause. *European Camping and Caravaning* is definitely recommended for pre-travel reading and is one of the best introductions to this mode of travel.

How to Camp Europe by Train

Lenore Baken
Mercer Island, Washington: Ariel Publications
$5.95, paperback, 384 pp., 1977, revised biennially

Purpose and Audience

How to Camp Europe by Train explains just that. This revised edition also includes a car-camping supplement and a rundown of the advantages and disadvantages of both modes of camping. It is aimed primarily at campers who want to save money by avoiding escalating gas prices and car rental fees. A hefty section of the book is devoted to travel preparation, train/motoring information, food, shopping strategies, etc. Chapters on fifteen Western European countries describe selected towns and cities and nearby campsites. Maps are included, as are occasional sight-seeing and restaurant suggestions.

What's Included

🧳 ✈ 🚂 🚗 ⛺ 🍴 🍶 🔩

Evaluation

Lenore Baken proposes a viable and inexpensive way to see Europe for Eurailpass or student railpass users. Although smaller towns receive ample coverage, the emphasis is on a "Grand Tour," major city approach. Especially helpful are the numerous maps, the specific directions to campsites from train stations, and the information for families traveling with children. One drawback is its rather complex organization and the apparent random selection of areas covered. All in all, though, this is a very useful guide for campers in Europe.

Motor Camping Around Europe

John Malo
Harrisburg, Pennsylvania: Stackpole Books
$6.95, paperback, 192 pp., 1975

Purpose and Audience

> *Motor Camping Around Europe* focuses on the preparation and practicalities of motor camping in nineteen Western European countries and Morocco. This is a "how to" guide, replete with all the basics, and not a directory to campsites. The emphasis is on touring in a trailer, but advice also applies to campers with cars and tents. Information on motoring, camping, campgrounds, and areas of interest is provided for the individual countries.

What's Included

Evaluation

> *Motor Camping* tends to emphasize the advantages of motor camping in Europe without discussing the disadvantages. The information is thorough and complete, but a bit wordy. *Motor Camping Around Europe* is best suited for neophyte travelers who desire a general introduction to this mode of travel. It will be helpful for pretravel reading but not of much use once on the road.

Rand McNally European Campground Guide*

Chicago: Rand McNally and Company
$6.95, paperback, 352 pp., 1977

Purpose and Audience

Rand McNally's multilingual directory lists over three thousand six hundred selected campsites in Europe. Forty-one points of information on each site, including address, activities, facilities, fees, etc., are arranged in tabular form across two pages, facilitating comparisons with other campsites. Instead of an alphabetical arrangement, the towns are listed in the order in which you would reach them if you traveled the main tourist routes.

What's Included

Evaluation

Other than the forty-one points of information on each site, no additional or supplemental information is supplied. Other guidebooks will have to be consulted for advice on camping and trailer travel, as well as for information and description of countries visited. Campgrounds have not been personally inspected; the information has been gleaned from extensive questionnaires sent to campground owners. An excellent feature of the Rand McNally guide is its atlas, which indicates where sites are located and also serves as a detailed road map. The "travel route" organization and tabular format may be confusing at first but, once mastered, render the book a useful tool for pretrip planning and on-the-road consultation.

*Rand McNally also publishes a companion *Road Atlas of Europe* containing maps of thirty-one countries and eighteen cities. It is distributed by Rand McNally for $3.95.

BICYCLING AND WALKING GUIDES

Bicycle Touring in Europe

Karen and Gary Hawkins
New York: Random House
$2.95, paperback, 184 pp., 1973

Purpose and Audience

Bicycle Touring in Europe is a handbook for both potential and experienced bikers. Over two-thirds of the book is devoted to the preparation and essential information necessary for bicycle touring. In addition, nine European tours are enticingly laid out, complete with basic maps and lists of youth hostels and principal campgrounds. *Bicycle Touring*, with the exception of the nine suggested tours, is not a guide to specific places. Rather, it instructs you how to plan and execute a European bicycle tour of your own choosing.

What's Included

Evaluation

Bicycle Touring is well written, well organized, and well worth the investment for experienced and neophyte bikers alike. Although written in 1973, it remains the best biking guide around. All the help and encouragement needed to plan and carry out a European bicycle tour is contained in an interesting narrative of suggestions and personal experiences. This guide is highly recommended for anyone intent on embarking on a bicycle tour of Europe.

Turn Right at the Fountain

George W. Oakes and Alexandra Chapman
New York: The New American Library
$1.75, paperback, 304 pp., 1973

Purpose and Audience

Turn Right at the Fountain is a "classic" guide to walking tours of European cities. First published in 1961, it has withstood eleven printings and is now in its third edition and yet is virtually unchanged. The author claims that the only way to get to know a city is by walking through it. These "guided" tours to twenty major European cities direct the traveler to both principle sights and more unusual, less-frequented spots. Turn Right at the Fountain has proven its appeal to a wide audience.

What's Included

Evaluation

Walking tours offer an interesting and rewarding way of seeing and experiencing European cities. The tours offer just enough information to satisfy the majority of interested travelers. Maps accompanied by clearly stated directions prevent confusion. Turn Right at the Fountain is recommended as a pleasant supplement to the more traditional restaurant and accommodation guides.

Walk Straight Through the Square: Walking Tours Through Europe's Most Picturesque Cities and Towns*

Juliann V. Skurdenis and Lawrence J. Smircich
New York: David McKay Company, Inc.
$4.95, paperback, 206 pp., 1976

Purpose and Audience

This is a guidebook with a very specific, limited goal: to get you to walk through and experience some of Europe's lesser-known cities and towns. In this jet age, the coauthors advocate this particular travel philosophy as an important part of European experience. One- to two-day walking tours are provided along with maps for twelve cities of France, Switzerland, Austria, Italy, and Yugoslavia.

What's Included

Evaluation

Unlike *Turn Right at the Fountain*, this guidebook avoids major cities and concentrates on less-frequented towns. For example, instead of covering Rome, Florence, and Venice, *Walk Straight Through the Square* provides walking tours for Assisi, Ravenna,

---

*A second book with the identical format has been written by the same authors:
More Walk Straight Through the Square
Juliann V. Skurdenis and Lawrence J. Smircich
New York: David McKay Company, Inc.
$4.95, paperback, 205pp., 1976

Siena, and Verona. This approach encourages exploration not only of major cities but also of the more important "typical" and "picturesque" areas that convey the national flavor. Tours include a bit of history of the town and country. This guide is recommended as a supplement to more practical guides and a sourcebook for potential trips.

Wandering: a Walker's Guide to the Mountain Trails of Europe

Ruth Rudner
New York: Dial Press
$3.95, paperback, 329 pp., 1972

Purpose and Audience

Wandering espouses an unusual way to experience Europe: walking through the mountains. Writing partially in diary form Ruth Rudner manages to combine her personal experiences and necessary practical information in an engaging narrative. This is more a "philosophy of wandering" guide than a guide to specific places. Walking tours are recounted for nine Western and Eastern European countries with an additonal chapter on a climbing school in Austria. *Wandering* is intended both for experienced hikers who have explored this mode of travel in the U.S. and novices who intend to start in Europe.

What's Included

Evaluation

>Ms. Rudner's account of her alpine adventures provides an excellent introduction to a potentially very satisfying European experience. Although a good amount of practical information is included, an authorative and inclusive handbook on hiking would be necessary for beginners. In addition, maps and specific instructions are also a prerequisite before one actually attempts an ascent. Highly recommended for an idea of what it is really like *before* you go.

Part Two
Africa

Introduction

The wave of interest in African travel seems to have hit around 1973 to 1975. Coupled with the increased number of travelers to Africa was a trend to venture into Sub-Saharan Africa as well as North Africa.

This is one area of the world where a guide is mandatory. The very qualities that contribute to Africa's exotic appeal necessitate forewarning and preparation. Without it, they too easily become dangerous.

Yet, despite the upswing in African travel, there is a relative paucity of guidebooks devoted to Africa. There are no annually revised guides for Africa as a whole other than the new Rand McNally *Africa Guide,* which with its 1977 publication date is one of two post-1975 guides to Africa available.

Although the publication dates of many of the guides render their information on prices, visa regulations, and even occasional country names obsolete, their quality is amazingly high. All of the Africa guides we cover provide good background reading and a sense of what to expect. The more complete guides can be updated with recent information obtained from embassies, etc. Another source of information on travel in Africa is the BIT Information and Help Service, 46 Great Western Road, London, W11, England.

Africa for the Hitchhiker

Fin Biering-Sorensen and Torben Jorgense
Copenhagen, Denmark: Bramsen and Hjort
$4.95, paperback, 159 pp., 1974
Distributed by CIEE, 777 United Nations Plaza, New York,
New York 10017

Purpose and Audience

Africa for the Hitchhiker is chiefly concerned with the practicalities of rock bottom travel in Africa. "Hitchhiking" is assumed to mean more than bumming rides; for the author it implies a very close contact with people in the countries where you travel. Other modes of travel such as trains, buses, etc., are therefore covered as well. A thorough introductory chapter is followed by six brief possible itineraries and a complete rundown on all countries in Africa.

What's Included

Evaluation

The focus on cheap travel excludes cultural, historical, or social information. This is a guide for practical matters—and the 1974 publication date jeopardizes its accuracy. Yet the authors convincingly convey the possibility of rock bottom travel in Africa, and a good deal of information might still be relevant. Good for pretravel reading, its small, compact format makes it easily portable for travel as well.

Africa Guide

Economist Intelligence Unit Ltd.
Essex, England: Africa Guide Co.
$14.95, paperback, 311 pp., revised annually
Distributed by Rand McNally & Co.

Purpose and Audience

Africa Guide is an annual publication that aims to provide a comprehensive and up-to-date presentation of important issues and facts about contemporary Africa. This is not a travel guide in the traditional sense; it is directed primarily at businessmen but also addresses government officials, journalists, researchers, and travelers. The guide begins with a series of articles concerning African political development, economy, social affairs, and travel. The "Country-by-Country" section includes a rundown on the history, economy, and political affairs of each country and a section concerned with travel and business.

What's Included

Evaluation

Although the *Africa Guide* is directed principally toward businessmen, the information contained would be of interest to other travelers as well. It will have great value as an annual publication, keeping abreast of conditions in an area where radical changes occur frequently. Its greatest asset is the section concerned with contemporary political Africa: the travel sections are somewhat brief and limited in scope.

Africa on the Cheap

Geoff Crowther
South Yarra, Victoria, Australia: Lonely Planet Publications
$3.95, paperback, 240 pp., 1977
Distributed by CIEE, 777 United Nations Plaza, New York, New York 10017

Purpose and Audience

With its 1977 publication date, *Africa on the Cheap*, along with Rand McNally's *Africa Guide,* is the most up-to-date guide on travel conditions in Africa. Covering fifty-two African nations, *Africa on the Cheap* was compiled by Geoff Crowther from his own African travel experiences and from the files of the legendary London underground travel service, BIT. Crowther's guide is designed for travelers seeing Africa on their own; it is a "how to" guide, covering every facet of African travel from visas and currency to hitching and health. It is interestingly written and packed with information on seeing Africa as inexpensively, intelligently, and safely as possible.

What's Included

Evaluation

Africa on the Cheap is a must for the adventurous low-budget traveler to Africa who will be seeing the continent without the dubious benefit of a guided tour.

Crowther's introduction gives a few simple tenets for successful African travel, reminding would-be African travelers to plan their schedules loosely, allowing for the unexpected, which may come in the form of washed-out roads in rainy season, delays in securing a hitch, or government bureaucracies. A good bibliography of other guides and books on Africa is included, as are excellent sections on visas and customs, transportation (seasonal road problems, hitching, overlanding, how to select and equip a vehicle), health, and rules of the road. These sections are followed by an alphabetical description of fifty-two African countries, each including a basic political history, geographical-climatic information, and specifics on visas, health certificates, currency, language(s), accommodations, and transport in the particular nation under discussion. *Africa on the Cheap* probably should be supplemented with a guide to sights, as this is where it is briefest and weakest; on all other facets of African travel it's superb.

Africa on Wheels: A Scrounger's Guide to Motoring in Africa

John J. Byrne
Newfoundland, New Jersey: Haessner Publishing, Inc.
$4.95, paperback, 160 pp., 1973

Purpose and Audience

For the person who prefers to do everything the hard way, this book tells how to travel clear across the African continent by motor vehicle with little danger and minimal expense. The author bases this book on his seven-month trek across Africa. This is not a guide in the traditional sense: no accommodations, restaurants, or sights in Africa are suggested. Instead, practical advice on how to take off on your own is provided along with personal anecdotes.

What's Included

Evaluation

Unlike many travel books, *Africa on Wheels* reads like a fascinating story yet manages to include very practical information. A thorough index directs you to the proper chapters, and handy appendixes isolate helpful hints. Despite the 1973 publication date, much of the information on how to travel overland in Africa remains relevant. *Africa on Wheels* is highly recommended as pretravel reading for potential overlanders and vagabonds in Africa.

Bright Continent: A Shoestring Guide to Sub-Saharan Africa

Susan Blumenthal
Garden City, New York: Doubleday and Company, Inc.
$5.95, paperback, 545 pp., 1974

Purpose and Audience

"For the tourist, vacationing student, businessman, journalist, Africanist, or armchair traveler, *Bright Continent* slices through the misconceptions and ignorance that have surrounded Sub-Saharan Africa—one of the last frontiers in international travel." This blurb from the dust cover of the book defines its contents very well. *Bright Continent* covers Sub-Saharan black Africa and white-ruled South Africa, leaving coverage of North Africa to other authors. Visas, health precautions, and transportation to and in Africa are amply discussed. The general tenor of the book exudes sympathy toward rock bottom and moderate-budget travelers but also includes listings for more luxurious restaurants and accommodations.

What's Included

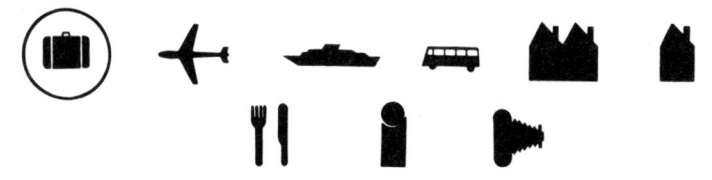

Evaluation

Bright Continent is a refreshing and practical guide to Africa, combining the best of traditional guides and personal narrative. Ms. Blumenthal clearly transmits her fascination, love, and deep respect for Africa. Especially interesting are her introductory comments concerning the historical background, cultural makeup, and flavor of each country. Major city maps aid in orientation and are a feature not frequently found in African guides. The frequent guidebook problem of out-of-date prices, addresses, and visa regulations unfortunately applies to *Bright Continent*. It has not been revised since publication in 1974. Despite this drawback, *Bright Continent* is highly recommended for pre-travel reading and use on the road for the budget-minded voyager.

East Africa: A Travel Guide

Alan Magary and Kerstin Fraser Magary
New York: Harper & Row Publishers
$6.95, paperback, 714 pp., 1975

Purpose and Audience

East Africa: A Travel Guide is a meticulously researched and excellent handbook for travel in Kenya, Tanzania, Malawi, Zambia, and Ethiopia. Based on a sixteen-month camping excursion, it is a thoroughly practical and interesting guide for East Africa. Information ranges from customs advice to tips on hitchhiking. The book addresses all manner of travelers and covers all the practicalities of East African travel, providing in addition ratings of hotels and restaurants and sight-seeing suggestions.

What's Included

Evaluation

It is difficult to imagine a more complete guide to East Africa. The Magarys write well and the guide should appeal to both armchair and potential travelers to Africa alike. The advice to campers and low-budget travelers is of special interest. *East Africa* is highly recommended for pretravel reading and would be indispensable once on the road. The only problem is its age: published in 1975, the prices listed are based on travel in 1973-1974.

The Traveler's Africa

Philip M. Allen and Aaron Segal
New York: Hopkinson & Blake
$14.95, hardback, 972 pp., 1973

Purpose and Audience

Here, in nearly one thousand pages, in the most comprehensive collection on historical, social, and travel-oriented facts about the entire African continent of fifty-seven countries. This guide addresses every kind of traveler—the rich, the budget-conscious, the adventurous, the student. *The Traveler's Africa* eschews traditional tourist jargon and philosophy and adopts a level-headed, and also interesting, style. Practicalities—ranging from beggars to hotel accommodations—are amply covered. Appendixes list educational tours and study programs at African universities, work, and service opportunities, conversion tables, etc.

What's Included

Evaluation

This major work on travel in Africa is at the top of its line. It is thoroughly researched, comprehensive, well organized, and, despite its weight and cost, an indispensable aid both before and during travel. Its 1973 publication date renders most accommodation and airline prices obsolete. However, a good deal of the material transcends time factors, and *The Traveler's Africa* remains highly recommended at this time.

Part Three
Asia

Introduction

The variety of guides to Asia is wide enough to meet most any traveler's needs. The standard tradition- and culture-oriented guides exist in the form of *The All-Asia Guide* and *Fodor's Southeast Asia*. In addition, there exist a large number of guides directed specifically to students, among them, *The On Your Own Guide to Asia* and *The Student Guide to Asia*. Finally, advice for the rock bottom traveler has been provided by Tony Wheeler in *South-East Asia on a Shoestring* and *Across Asia on the Cheap*. See also *The Traveler's Guidebook to Europe and Asia: Your Passport to Making It Abroad* which is reviewed in the chapter on Europe: Speciality Guides. Happily, many of these guides are revised annually or are at least fairly current.

Another source of information on travel abroad in Asia is the BIT Information and Help Service, 46 Great Western Road, London, W11, England. BIT publishes a mimeographed book, *Overland to India and Australia*, which, unfortunately, we were not able to review.

Across Asia on the Cheap

Tony Wheeler
South Yarra, Victoria, Australia: Lonely Planet Publications*
$2.75, paperback, 144 pp., 1975, revised periodically
Distributed by Bookpeople, 2940 Seventh Street, Berkeley, California 94710

Purpose and Audience

Across Asia on the Cheap is intended for people traveling overland from Australia or New Zealand westward across Asia to Europe. The author, a seasoned rock bottom traveler, suggests that eastbound travelers simply read the guide backward. Prices are generally listed in both Australian and U.S. dollars. Essentially a "how to" travel guide, almost one-third of the book is devoted to preparatory information. Information on the twelve major countries covered includes principal sights, history, travel conditions, visas, food and essential vocabulary. *Across Asia* is for the "subbudget," i.e., rock bottom overland traveler.

What's Included

*Other publications of Lonely Planet Publications are
  Africa On the Cheap
  Australia: A Traveller's Survival Kit
  Europe: A Traveller's Survival Kit
  Nepal: A Traveller's Guide
  New Zealand: A Travel Survival Kit
  South-East Asia On A Shoestring
  Trekking in the Himalayas

ASIA

Evaluation

This guide, based on the author's own travel adventures, is most useful for pretravel reading. It advocates a rock bottom budget travel style and leaves much up to the individual. A few specific hotels are mentioned (without addresses) but more often than not the traveler is directed to an area with the largest number of inexpensive hotels. *Across Asia* makes for interesting reading and is a good introduction to overland travel, but it is not necessarily indispensable once on the road.

All-Asia Guide

Michael Westlake, Editor
Rutland, Vermont: Charles E. Tuttle Company, Inc.
$5.95, paperback, 544 pp., revised annually
For sale in North and South America and Japan only.

Purpose and Audience

The *All-Asia Guide* is just that. It covers twenty-seven Asian countries, including both Chinas and even Mongolia. It purports to address both expense account travelers *and* students. The guide has a great deal of practical information, maps, and historical and cultural material in a surprisingly compact fomat. Addresses, phone numbers, and rates are listed for accommodations, which are also rated by the guide.

What's Included

🧳 ✈️ 🚂 🏭 🏠 🍴 🛏️ 🔌

Evaluation

The *All-Asia Guide* is sponsored by the *Far Eastern Economic Review* which in part explains its "expense account" orientation. Indeed, most accommodations suggested are beyond a student's budget. It is, however, the most complete in-depth guide to Asia. Helpful maps are also an asset. This book is highly recommended for use with another student guide, such as *The Student Guide to Asia* or *The On Your Own Guide to Asia*.

Fodor's Southeast Asia

Eugene Fodor and Robert C. Fisher, Editors
New York: David McKay Company
$12.95, hardback, 511 pp., 1977, revised periodically

Purpose and Audience

Fodor's Southeast Asia continues the Fodor tradition of high-quality guides. Covering thirteen Southeast Asian countries, introductory chapters concentrate on the Asian travel scene, describing transportation, culture, history, and religion. They are followed by individual country chapters. Budget is not a concern and most prices apply to moderate-budget travelers.

What's Included

Evaluation

As with the other Fodor Guides, the emphasis is on background and sights, with less attention paid to accommodation and restaurant listings. The advantages of Fodor's over other Asian guides, even the *All-Asia Guide,* is its thoroughly interesting and extremely practical introduction to Asian culture, which integrates etiquette for travelers with cultural observations. This guide is very highly recommended for travelers to Southeast Asia, both for pretravel reading and for on-the-spot consultation.

Myro Waldo's Travel Guide to the Orient and the Pacific

New York: Macmillan Publishing Co., Inc.
$7.95, paperback, 712 pp., 1977, revised biennially

Purpose and Audience

Myra Waldo tackles the Orient in her usual fashion. Here she covers twenty-three countries. Sixty-five pages of introduction are quite thorough for the traveler of above moderate means but lack tips and information for the budget-conscious traveler. As befits the Orient, a great deal of attention is paid to background information, sights, etc. Myra Waldo also lingers on the special attractions and unique features of each country.

What's Included

🧳 ✈ 🚢 🚂 🏠 🍴
🚪 🔌

Evaluation

Myra Waldo's Travel Guide to the Orient and the Pacific is clearly the best of the series. She provides introductory travel information that is difficult to find in other Asian guides, i.e., information on weather, International Date Line, etc. In addition, her rambling, discursive descriptions of sights and areas in this case disclose information not readily available elsewhere. While the restaurants and accommodations are well beyond rock bottom and moderate-budget travelers' means, *Myra Waldo's Guide to the Orient and the Pacific* is helpful for travel planning and preparation.

The On-Your-Own Guide to Asia

Philip McLeod, Editor
Stanford, California: Volunteers in Asia, Inc., and Rutland, Vermont: Charles E. Tuttle Co., Inc.
$3.95 , paperback, 288 pp., 1977

Purpose and Audience

The On-Your-Own Guide to Asia draws upon the experience of dozens of young travelers who, as members of Volunteers in Asia, have worked and lived in Asia for extended periods of time. The guide is directed to other students with limited budgets and concentrates on essential information for low-cost travel to ten countries in East and Southeast Asia. Relevant background information on history and culture is coupled with specific hotel and restaurant listings and transportation information.

What's Included

Evaluation

A very sensible guide to Asia, this compact book provides the essentials for low-cost travel in Asia. Especially helpful are the maps, bibliographies, and directions for major airports. This guide pleasantly eschews traditional tourist jargon for straightforward, practical advice. As it covers only ten Asian countries, it often provides more thorough and in-depth information than *The Student Guide to Asia*. *On-Your-Own* is a good introduction to the countries of Southern and Southeast Asia but should be supplemented by other guides in the suggested bibliographies for those desiring more in-depth knowledge. Good for both pretravel and travel use.

Pacific Paradise on a Low Budget

Charles and Carolyn Plank
Washington, D.C.: Acropolis Books
$3.50, paperback, 159 pp., 1973

Purpose and Audience

Pacific Paradise on a Low Budget proves that low-cost travel is not limited to the young. Written by an adventuresome retired couple, the book relates the Planks' travels in the South Pacific and Japan. A "how to guide" combined with an account of their own travels, *Pacific Paradise* opens new possibilities on how to plan and carry out low-cost travel in normally expensive areas.

What's Included

Evaluation

This is not a directory of places to stay or eat. The Planks' accounts of their extensive travels in Hong Kong, Japan, the Fiji Islands, Tonga, and Samoas will ease the way for similarly destined travelers. Their enthusiasm is contagious and their advice is excellent. Although prices quoted by the Planks are out of date, their "travel philosophy" certainly is not. *Pacific Paradise* is recommended for pretravel reading but not for use once on the road.

South-East Asia on a Shoestring

Tony Wheeler
South Yarra, Victoria, Australia: Lonely Planet Publications
$2.50, paperback, 149 pp., 1977, revised biennially
Distributed by Bookpeople, 2940 Seventh Street, Berkeley, California 94710

Purpose and Audience

South-East Asia on a Shoestring is a handy little guide to the rock bottom travel in eight Southeast Asian countries. It complements and continues the tradition of another guide by the same author, *Across Asia on the Cheap*. Most practical matters are covered, including transportation, hotel-restaurant suggestions, visas, etc.

What's Included

🧳 ✈ 🚢 🏠 ▶

Evaluation

Although budget concerns are a priority, Tony Wheeler manages to include some cultural and historical information as well as solid information on rock bottom travel in Asia. Among the book's assets are its portability and low cost. It is also an Australian publication, perhaps not as well known to American subbudget vagabonds as other publications. On the other hand, some of the information is sketchy at best, and addresses are often incomplete. *South-East Asia on a Shoestring* would make a good supplement to a more inclusive culture- and sight-oriented book such as the *All-Asia Guide*.

The Student Guide to Asia

David Jenkins and the Australian Union of Students
New York: E.P. Dutton and Company, Inc.
$3.95, paperback, 320 pp., 1977, revised biennially

Purpose and Audience

This guide is for Asia what *Let's Go* is for Europe: a student-oriented, budget survey guide to twenty-five countries in Asia. Written by the Australian Union of Students, *The Student Guide to Asia* provides a capsule history of each country, followed by its vital statistics, currency and visa requirements, and a rundown on culture, transport systems, and places to see. A directory of accommodations is concentrated in one section; local foods are discussed, but no specific restaurant recommendations are included.

What's Included

Evaluation

> *The Student Guide to Asia* suffers many of the problems and offers many of the advantages of the European *Let's Go*. While its inclusive broad coverage of all of Asia suits the student traveler intent on voyaging great distances, it necessarily limits the depth of treatment of individual countries. General introductory remarks are very brief, just touching the principal points of travel in Asia. Likewise, travel across and to Asia from Europe and Australia is summarized in two pages. *The Student Guide to Asia* provides essential information for travel but lacks a more comprehensive "travel philosophy" and preparatory information.

Part Four
South America

Introduction

South America is a likely destination for the veteran traveler who has been to Europe several times. And more and more adventurous travelers are heading south of the border—before heading west. Realizing this potential tourist market, the major series guides like Fodor's and Frommer's are publishing annually or biennially revised guides for South America.

The long-established classic guide to South America, considered the "bible" by many experienced travelers, is *The South American Handbook*. It is the only guide reviewed that also covers both Central America and Mexico.

Price obsolesence in guides to South America is a serious problem with escalating inflation. All guides included here are published annually, which helps somewhat in making cost estimates. Note also that the only guide directed specifically to students is *The Student Guide to Latin America*, although *The South American Handbook* also indicates low-budget to rock bottom accommodations.

The American Automobile Association (AAA) also publishes infrequently revised guides for Mexico and Central and South America.

Fodor's South America

Eugene Fodor and Robert C. Fisher, Editors
New York: David McKay Company, Inc.
$9.95, paperback, 621 pp., revised annually

Purpose and Audience

Fodor's tackles the thirteen countries of South America in an assiduously thorough guide. A substantial introduction to the continent and a practical section on pretrip planning are followed by material introducing each of the individual countries. Although most of the information is geared toward the moderate- and high-budget traveler, care is also taken to include the low-budget traveler.

What's Included

Evaluation

The tone of Fodor's South America's introductory and background material is more tourist-oriented and chatty than the more scholarly South American Handbook. Fodor's reliance on country specialists to write the individual country chapters invites a wide range of opinion. All in all, Fodor's South America is a very good introduction to this less-traveled continent and very highly recommended. It is especially useful for background information and as a guide to larger and capital cities; it is somewhat weaker on smaller cities.

Myra Waldo's Travel Guide to South America

New York: Macmillan Publishing Company, Inc.
$8.95, paperback, 422 pp., 1976

Purpose and Audience

Myra Waldo candidly offers her own personal, subjective guide to South America. The guide is directed to those who can debate the advantages and disadvantages of first-class versus tourist plane travel. This is *not* the guide for student and budget travelers. Coverage of the ten major South American countries focuses on capital cities, with only limited information on surrounding areas, cities, and sights.

What's Included

▪ ✈ ⛴ 🏛 🍴 🍷 ▶

Evaluation

First written in 1972, This "revised" edition does not appear to have been updated all that much. Restaurant and hotel listings do not include addresses and are well beyond most budget—even moderate—travelers' realm of possibilities. Some, however, may enjoy the chatty, informal, and occasionally humorous accounts of South America's history, peoples, and current political situations. But take them with a grain of salt, since they are written from a naive and patronizing point of view. For those interested in a more in-depth and objective approach, both *The South American Handbook* and *Fodor's South America* are far superior.

South America on $10 and $15 a Day

Arnold and Harriet Greenberg
New York: Arthur Frommer, Inc.
$4.50, paperback, 367 pp., revised biennially
Distributed by Simon and Schuster

Purpose and Audience

South America on $10 and $15 a Day continues the Frommer tradition of providing a wide selection of low- to moderate-budget accommodations and restaurants. Like the other guides of this series, the *South America* guide sticks to coverage of capital cities. This edition also includes coverage of Salvador and the ruins of San Augustin, as well as Panama City.

What's Included

🧳 ✈ 🏭 🏠 🍴 📖 🗝

Evaluation

As the title indicates, the book is geared to low- and moderate-budget travelers. Cost estimates include *only* hotel and three meals a day. The emphasis is on "creature comforts," although sights are also included. For more in-depth information on historical, cultural, and social background, see either *Fodor's South America* or *The South American Handbook*.

The South American Handbook

John Brooks, Editor
Bath, England: Trade and Travel Publications, Ltd.
$16.95, hardback, 1032 pp., revised annually
Distributed by Rand McNally and Company

Purpose and Audience

Published in England but adapted for American travelers, *The South American Handbook* purports to address all visitors, whether "sightseers or businessmen." This fifty-third revised edition now includes coverage of all Caribbean Islands, Mexico, and Central and South America. This well-organized guide covers every practical detail for travel in South America, in addition to a rundown on its peoples, history, and present forms of government.

What's Included

Evaluation

A maximum of information is packed into a relatively small format. Although it is very expensive, this guidebook is invaluable for travelers who desire more than the standard, tourist-oriented jargon and are headed for less well known areas and islands. While budget accommodations are included, the general orientation and travel philosophy does not lean in the direction of rock bottom budgets. And the editors warn of escalating inflation, which can render most prices obsolete as soon as the book goes to press. Despite the drawbacks of high cost for the guidebook itself and potentially obsolete price listings, *The South American Handbook* is exceptional in its breadth of coverage. It is highly recommended for travelers who desire a knowledge of the history and cultural makeup of each country and a greater understanding of contemporary South America.

The Student Guide to Latin America

Council on International Educational Exchange
New York: E. P. Dutton & Co., Inc.
$2.95, paperback, 149 pp., 1977

Purpose and Audience

Written by the Council on International Educational Exchange and oriented toward student travelers, this guidebook covers Mexico and Central and South America. It is not a "how to" travel guide; only the essential information is included. A general introduction relays the basics on transportation to Latin America and health and money considerations. The alphabetically organized country chapters offer an introduction to the lands and peoples of Latin America as well as information on travel options. Individual city and area headings include hotel and restaurant listings as well as other travel information.

SOUTH AMERICA

What's Included

Evaluation

The Student Guide to Latin America does not aim for thoroughness but rather concentrates on budget prices. In-depth coverage is not to be found: countries are usually covered in approximately ten pages. Within the above limitations, this guidebook will direct you to the best buys and cheapest hotels. However, even major cities are covered superficially and many areas are not covered at all. Coupled with *The South American Handbook,* as the authors suggest, the result is a dynamic duo: extensive coverage of Latin and South America on a minimal budget.

Part Five
Worldwide

Introduction

It is certainly possible today to circumnavigate the world in less than eighty days. Speed and good travel are not always fine bedfellows and many guides in this chapter offer worldwide travel at a slower pace. For example, consider traveling around the world on four wheels, as *Overlanding* suggests, or even by train, as *Fodor's Railways of the World* outlines. These guides focus on a specific mode of travel. Other guides, such as *Pan Am's World Guide* or *Rand McNally Traveler's Almanac* concentrate on statistics, facts, and travel regulations for countries around the world.

Ford's Freighter Travel Guide*

Merrian E. Clark, Editor and Publisher
Woodland Hills, California: Ford's Travel Guides
$4.50, paperback, revised semiannually—March and September

Purpose and Audience

Published semiannually, Ford's Freighter Travel Guide will tell you what freighter's sailing where and how to get aboard it. The book is organized by port of departure and gives descriptions of the ships and price of passage. It is a complete and up-to-date reference directory to freighter travel.

What's Included

Evaluation

Ford's Freighter Travel Guide has a brief "Introduction to Freighter Travel" that covers the essentials efficiently and concisely. The book is extremely well organized and easy to use. Its excellent index of ports of call and the lines that serve them includes a listing number for easy cross-reference with the "Passenger Carrying Freighter" section, which is organized by port of departure. A handy index lists ports of the world by country and world maps with port cities indicated to facilitate travel planning. This is a very useful tool for anyone contemplating a freighter journey.

*Ford's also publishes a Ford's International Cruise Guide semiannually—May and October. Like the Ford's Freighter Travel Guide, it is a directory of cruise ship information and includes information on price of passage and descriptions of the ships.

Fodor's Cruises Everywhere 1977

Eugene Fodor and Robert C. Fisher, Editors
New York: David McKay Co., Inc.
$9.95, paperback, 366 pp., revised annually

Purpose and Audience

Fodor's Cruises Everywhere 1977 is the first edition of an annually revised guide to cruises. Although cruising is probably out of the price range of the student or low- or moderate-budget traveler, Fodor's cruise guide properly suggests that the average cruise cost of $50-70 a day (including three-plus gourmet meals) is best compared to costs for an elegant land-based resort. For those who can foot that bill, *Cruises Everywhere 1977* is a very complete guide to the waterways of the world and the ships that cruise them. The one area not covered is Africa, since the editors felt that political conditions and cruise itineraries were too uncertain at the time of writing to warrant inclusion in the present edition.

What's Included

Evaluation

Like other Fodor's Guides, *Cruises Everywhere* is well researched and thorough. Its ninety-page introduction to cruises includes helpful information on planning, money-saving ideas, and an excellent picture of luxurious shipboard life—a feature helpful to those who are still deciding on whether a cruise is the vacation they're seeking. The introduction also addresses the concerns of the single cruise traveler and of retired persons. In a section entitled "World Cruises Areas," *Fodor's Cruises Everywhere* gives an overview of costs, the best time of year to go, and what ports to visit for each of the cruise areas identified. Another section describes representative cruises, and the guide concludes with extensive sections on individual ports, shipping lines and their ships, and a 1977 schedule of cruises. Expected yearly updates should keep this a current and useful volume, especially when supplemented with a guide to the ports to be visited.

Fodor's Railways of the World

Rogers W. M. Whitaker, Robert C. Fisher, and Leslie Brown,
Editors
New York: David McKay Company, Inc.
$9.95, paperback, 374 pp., 1977

Purpose and Audience

Fodor's Railways of the World addresses experienced and inexperienced train travelers alike. This is a guide to train travel in one hundred and one countries on the six continents. Not a schedule (use *Thomas Cook International Time Table* for European train schedules), this guide explains the "ins and outs" and "how tos" of train travel. *Fodor's Railways of the World* gives a country-by-country rundown on the state of train travel, important addresses, and a review of train travel service.

WORLDWIDE

What's Included

Evaluation

Fodor's Railways of the World makes informative reading and serves as an introduction to this justifiably time-honored mode of travel. Serving as a solid introduction to trains not only in the U.S.A. and Europe, but worldwide, it allows the intrepid traveler to expand itinerary possibilities. Well-organized, thorough, and informative, *Fodor's Railways* is recommended for pre-travel reading.

The Freighter Travel Manual

Bradford Angier
Radnor, Pennsylvania: Chilton Book Co.
$3.95, paperback, 248 pp., 1974

Purpose and Audience

Bradford Angier tries to show that travel by freighter provides many of the amenities of cruise ship travel without the high price tag. That is not to say that it is inexpensive. Would-be freighter travelers need a good deal of money and a flexible time schedule: freighters often make unscheduled stops to pick up and discharge cargo, which is, after all, their main business. The book contains chapters on preparation, seagoing orientation, information on U.S. customs regulations, and a section on ports of interest.

What's Included

Evaluation

The Freighter Travel Manual was published in 1974, and readers should beware of much of its "date-sensitive" information, such as visa, duty, and innoculation information, as well as prices quoted. Although Angier bills his book as a "manual," it is not terribly practical as a "how to" book. There is an entire chapter devoted to preparation, but it centers on how to close your house, stop the mail, and the like rather than on how to get ready for your freighter journey. Similarly, much of the information provided under promising chapter headings like "Basic Health Precautions," "At Home on the Ocean," or "Shipboard Pastimes," is poorly focused or downright questionable—advising you to get a fluoride treatment for your teeth before you leave, a permanent (if you're a woman), or enumerating what minerals are found in salt water or the rules for shuffleboard. It would certainly have to be supplemented by a guide to the ports to be visited. *The Freighter Travel Manual* will interest those who want to learn more about interpreting weather signs at sea or get a feeling for nautical terminology or the leisurely and luxurious pace of freighter life. It will not steer you to specific ships or direct you to the different freighter lines. Those who are after a more practical approach would do better with *Ford's Freighter Travel Guide.*

How to Travel Without Being Rich

Norman D. Ford
Greenlawn, New York: Harian Publications
$2.50, paperback, 170 pp., 1976

Purpose and Audience

This is a guide for worldwide travel at "stay-at-home" prices. Norman Ford, author of many guidebooks, advocates cheap travel on age-old trade and caravan routes. Ford provides the "how tos" for finding travel bargains and supplies the specifics for trans-Atlantic travel, etc. In addition, itineraries for continental and round-the-world travel are suggested.

What's Included

Evaluation

This guidebook fills a gap in travel literature: low-cost travel tips that cross geographic and continental boundaries. The same glib, overconfident style that characterizes most of Ford/Harian publications is evident here, but it is balanced by much practical information. This guide certainly will be of interest for pretravel planning for world wide or transcontinental travelers.

Off the Beaten Track: A Wexas Travel Handbook

Ingrid Cranfield and Richard Harrington, Editors
London: Wexas International Limited
$9.95, paperback, 255 pp., 1977
Distributed by World Expeditionary Association, North American Office, Graybar Building, Suite 354, 420 Lexington Avenue, New York, New York 10017

Purpose and Audience

If you're planning an expedition or want to join one, *Off the Beaten Track* is the book for which you've been searching. Wexas, the World Expeditionary Society, was founded in London in 1970 to provide an information and travel service for expeditions. *Off the Beaten Track* tackles just about every aspect of expedition planning imaginable. Additionally, it provides lists of adventure trip operators in the United Kingdom, expeditions, and an annotated bibliography of books and periodicals concerned with off-the-beaten-track travel.

What's Included

Evaluation

Although Wexas has a New York as well as London base, *Off the Beaten Track* is distinctly British in orientation. Its British bias is well justified, however, by the fact that many of the best expeditions do, in fact, originate in England. Nevertheless, despite listings of worldwide expedition services, non-British readers may find the book somewhat less useful than their British or continental counterparts. *Off the Beaten Track* provides thorough and interesting information on expedition planning. The individual chapters are written by experts in the field, who contribute first-hand experience in such diverse facets of expedition planning as fund raising, map reading, and government bureaucracies. Sections on health care and photography will be of interest to all travelers to out-of-the-way places. The annotated bibliographies are encyclopedic in scope and will serve both those with an academic and those with a practical interest in expeditions. *Off the Beaten Track* will also steer you toward organizations that, like Wexas, run adventure trips. *Off the Beaten Track* is not directed toward those planning to take off for the wilds on their own, although some of its information would apply. But it is a unique reference work on expedition travel, well written and complete.

Overlanding: How to Explore the World on Four Wheels

John Steele Gordon
New York: Harper & Row Publishers
$4.95, paperback, 328 pp., 1975

Purpose and Audience

"Overlanding is the land lovers equivalent of sailing; the long, slow crossing of large areas of the world" by motor vehicle, preferably one with four-wheel drive. This challenging mode of travel is only for the adventurous and hardy. *Overlanding* is packed with instructions on preparation and execution of long-distance voyages. Not a guide to specific places, the book concentrates on practicalities that apply to all countries.

What's Included

Evaluation

As much a philosophy of travel as a transportation guide, the book covers both the practical and subjective aspects of overlanding. Not many guides exist for this special mode of travel, and this guide is extremely well researched and documented in all aspects of overlanding. Especially good are sections on preparations. Unfortunately, inflation has rendered the prices listed obsolete. Nonetheless, *Overlanding* is invaluable for potential overlanders, both for pretravel reading and reference once on the road.

Pan Am's World Guide: The Encyclopedia of Travel*

New York: McGraw-Hill Book Co.
$6.95, hardback, 1050 pp., 1976

Purpose and Audience

Intended as an authoritative reference for the prospective traveler to any part of the world, Pan Am's encyclopedia covers one hundred and forty-one countries. Its all-encompassing nature necessitates brevity. The country chapters are comprised of "general" background information and statistics, information on currency, and restaurant, accommodation, and sight recommendations. Pan Am routes and air travel times serve as transportation information to specific countries. Directed at the commercial airline user, suggested prices fall into the moderate-to-expensive range.

What's Included

Evaluation

Considering the scope of the book, the material is well organized, concise, and fairly complete. The information, however, does not go beyond a traditional tourist orientation. This guide should suffice for a stopover or

---

*Subsections of this book are published as separate books:
  Pan Am's Guide to Europe
  Pan Am's Guide to the Pacific
  Pan Am's Guide to Latin America
  U.S.A. Guide

short visit to major cities. More specialized guides should be consulted for longer stays.

Rand McNally Traveler's Almanac: The International Guide

Nancy Meyer, Editor
Los Angeles: Bill Muster
$6.95, paperback, 320 pp., revised annually
Distributed by Rand McNally and Company

Purpose and Audience

The *Traveler's Almanac* is a planning guide—not a guidebook. It is composed of a series of articles treating subjects ranging from air travel to vagabonding and attempts to fulfill the needs of wealthy and budget-conscious travelers alike. In addition to chapters on different travel modes and philisophies, the worldwide touring guide chapter details the practicalities of travel to some two hundred foreign destinations and includes general information on transportation, accommodations, foods, and entertainment.

What's Included

Evaluation

Pan Am's World Guide presents a good deal more specific information on individual countries than does *Rand McNally Traveler's Almanac*. Pan Am, however, does not include the series of articles introducing different travel possibilities, such a vagabonding. For the novice voyager, the *Traveler's Almanac* presents a wide range of such travel modes. Helpful features are the thorough index and the specific book suggestions for more in-depth information.

Whole World Handbook: A Student Guide to Work, Study, and Travel Abroad

Council on International Educational Exchange
New York: CIEE and Frommer/Pasmantier Publishing Corporation
$3.95, paperback, 368 pp., revised biennially

Purpose and Audience

In its fourth edition and new compact size, the *Whole World Handbook* remains an important clearinghouse of information, ideas, and addresses for short-term or long-term travel, work or study abroad. Directed to students, the *Handbook* is organized by area with essential information and specifics on individual countries. It is not a guidebook as such; travel information is only one of the topics covered by the *Handbook*.

What's Included

Evaluation

>Intended to be used in the United States before leaving, the *Whole World Handbook* is packed with information and is well organized and comprehensive. A resource for literally hundreds of names and addresses, the *Whole World Handbook* is one of the best books available on work, study, and travel opportunities around the world. The authors put forth a wide range of suggestions without pretending to have all the answers. For student travelers, the *Handbook* is top-flight reference to other guidebooks.

Appendixes

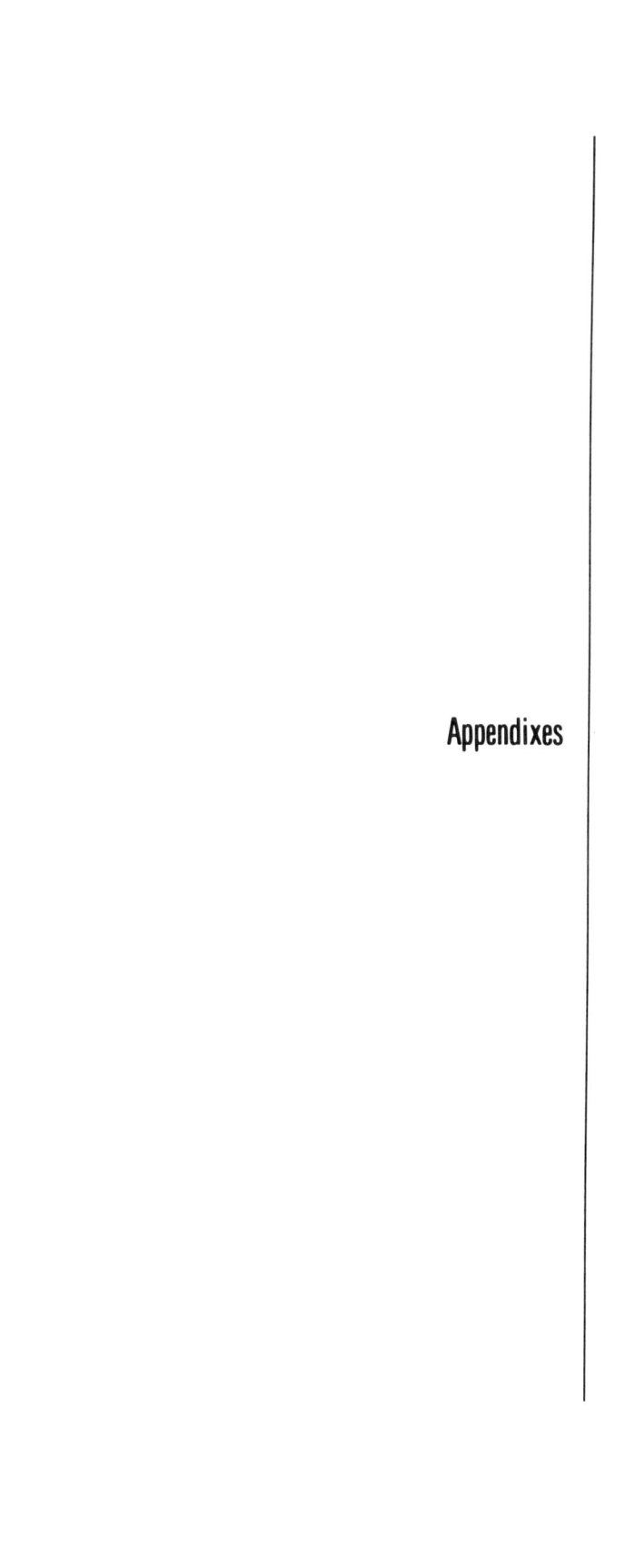

APPENDIX I

Alphabetical List of All Books

A to Z World Travel Guides, 45
AA Budget Guide to Europe, 67
AA Guide to Camping and Caravaning on the Continent, 87
AA Guide to Continental Motoring, 88
AAA European Accommodations, 68
AAA Travel Guide to Europe, 89
Across Asia on the Cheap, 125
Africa for the Hitchhiker, 111
Africa Guide, 112
Africa On the Cheap, 113
Africa on Wheels: A Scrounger's Guide to Motoring in Africa, 115
All-Asia Guide, 126
Arthur Frommer's Guides, 46

APPENDIX I

Baxter's Eurailpass Travel Guide, 79
Berlitz Travel Guides, 48
Bicycle Touring in Europe, 101
Blue Guides, 50
Bright Continent: A Shoestring Guide to Sub-Saharan Africa, 116
Castle Hotels of Europe, 69
Country Inns and Back Roads, European Edition, 70
Dollar Wise Guides, 52
East Africa: A Travel Guide, 117
Enjoy Europe by Car, 90
Enjoy Europe by Train, 80
Eurail Guide: How to Travel Europe by Train, 81
Europa Camping and Caravaning, 91
Europa Touring: Motoring Guide of Europe, 93
Europe by Eurail, 82
Europe on $10 a Day, 25
European Camping and Caravaning, 94
Fielding's Guide to Traveling with Children in Europe, 35
Fielding's Low-Cost Europe, 26
Fielding's Selected Favorites: Hotels and Inns, Europe, 71
Fielding's Travel Guide to Europe, 27
Fodor's Cruises Everywhere 1977, 150
Fodor's Europe, 29
Fodor's Guides, 53
Fodor's Railways of the World, 151
Fodor's South America, 139
Fodor's Southeast Asia, 127
Ford's Freighter Travel Guide and Ford's International Cruise Guide, 149
The Freighter Travel Manual, 152
Holdiay Travel Guides, 56
How to Camp Europe by Train, 95
How to Travel Without Being Rich, 154
International Youth Hostel Handbook: Volume I, Europe and Mediterranean Countries, 72
Let's Go: The Budget Guide to Europe, 30
Michelin Green Guides (English Editions), 57

Michelin Red Guides, 73
Motor Camping Around Europe, 96
Myra Waldo's Travel and Motoring Guide to Europe, 31
Myra Waldo's Travel Guide to South America, 140
Myra Waldo's Travel Guide to the Orient and the Pacific, 129
Nagel's Encyclopedia-Guides, 59
Off the Beaten Track: A Wexas Travel Handbook, 155
The On-Your-Own Guide to Asia, 130
Overlanding: How to Explore the World on Four Wheels, 157
Pacific Paradise on a Low Budget, 131
Pan Am's World Guide: The Encyclopedia of Travel, 158
Rand McNally European Campground Guide, 97
Rand McNally Traveler's Almanac: The International Guide, 159
The South American Handbook, 142
South America on $10 and $15 a Day, 141
South-East Asia on a Shoestring, 132
The Special Guide to Europe, 36
The Student Guide to Asia, 133
The Student Guide to Latin America, 143
Student Hostels and Tour Activities: Handbook for the Young Traveler, 74
Sunset Travel Guides, 61
The Traveler's Africa, 119
Traveler's Guide Book to Europe and Asia: Your Passport to Making It Abroad, 37
The Traveller's Survival Kit: Europe, 39
Turn Right at the Fountain, 102
Walk Straight Through the Square and *More Walk Straight Through the Square*, 103
Wandering: A Walker's Guide to the Mountain Trails of Europe, 104
Whitman's Off-Season Travel Guide to Europe, 40
Whole World Handbook: A Student Guide to Work, Study and Travel Abroad, 160
Youth Hosteler's Guide to Europe, 41
$10-A-Day Guides, 62

Appendix II

Names and Addresses of All Publishers and Distributors of Books Reviewed

Acropolis Books
  2400 17th Street, N.W., Courtyard,
  Washington, D.C. 20009

Africa Guide Company
  Distributed by Rand McNally & Company

American Automobile Association
  8111 Gatehouse Road
  Falls Church, Virginia 22042

American Map Company
  1926 Broadway
  New York, New York 10023

American Youth Hostels
National Campus
Delaplane, Virginia 22025
Distributors in the U.S.A. for International Youth Hostel Federation

Ariel Publications
P.O. Box 255
Mercer Island, Washington 98040

Arthur Frommer, Inc.
380 Madison Avenue
New York, New York 10017

The Automobile Association
P.O. Box 52
Basingstoke Hants, England
Distributed in the U.S.A. by Standing Orders, Inc.

Ernest Benn, Ltd.
Distributed in the U.S.A. by Rand McNally & Company

Berkshire Traveler Press
Pine Street
Stockbridge, Massachusetts 01262

Bookpeople
2940 Seventh Street
Berkeley, California 94710

Bramsen & Hjort
Distributed in the U.S.A. by Council on International Educational Exchange

Chilton Book Company
King of Prussia Road
Radnor, Pennsylvania 19087

Council of International Educational Exchange (CIEE)
777 United Nations Plaza
New York, New York 10017
Distributors in the U.S.A. for Bramsen & Hjort and the Swiss Student Travel Office

APPENDIX II

Dial Press
 1 Dag Hammarskjold Plaza
 245 East 47th Street
 New York, New York 10017

Doubleday & Company
 501 Franklin Avenue
 Garden City, New York 11530

Drake Publishers, Inc.
 801 2nd Avenue
 New York, New York 10017

Drei Brunnen Verlag
 7 Stuttgart 80 (Vaihingen)
 Postfach 80 0830 Germany
 Distributed in the U.S.A. by Europa Camping and Caravaning

E. P. Dutton & Company, Inc.
 201 Park Avenue, South
 New York, New York 10003

Editions Berlitz, S.A.
 13 Ave. de Jordils
 1000 Lausanne 6
 Switzerland
 Distributed in the U.S.A. by Macmillan Publishing Company, Inc.

Europa Camping and Caravaning
 2306 Sixth Street
 Clay Center, Kansas 67432

George Wright Ferguson
 Box 20334
 Columbus, Ohio 43220

Fielding Publications
   William Morrow & Company, Inc.
   105 Madison Avenue
   New York, New York 10016

Ford's Travel Guides
   P.O. Box 505
   22151 Clarendon Street
   Woodland Hills, California 91365

Arthur Frommer, Inc.
   380 Madison Avenue
   New York, New York 10017

Frommer/Pasmantier Publishing Corporation
   380 Madison Avenue
   New York, New York 10017

Haessner Publishing, Inc.
   Drawer B
   Newfoundland, New Jersey 07435

Hallwag Verlag
   Distributed in the U.S.A. by American Map Company

Harian Publications
   1000 Prince Street
   Greenlawn, New York 11740

Harper & Row Publishers
   10 East 53rd Street
   New York, New York 10022

Hastings House, Publishers, Inc.
   10 East 40th Street
   New York, New York 10016

Hippocrene Books, Inc.
   171 Madison Avenue
   New York, New York 10016

APPENDIX II

Hopkinson & Blake
    185 Madison Avenue
    New York, New York 10016

International Youth Hostel Federation
    Distributed by American Youth Hostels

Lane Publishing Company
    Willow & Middlefield Roads
    Menlo Park, California 94025

Lonely Planet Publications
    P.O. Box 88
    South Yarra, Victoria
    3141 Australia
    Distributed in the U.S.A. by Bookpeople

Robert P. Long
    634 Bellmore Avenue
    East Meadow, New York 11554

Macmillan Publishing Company, Inc.
    866 3rd Avenue
    New York, New York 10022

McGraw Hill Book Company
    1221 Avenue of the Americas
    New York, New York 10020

David McKay Company, Inc.
    750 3rd Avenue
    New York, New York 10017

Michelin Tire Corporation
    P.O. Box 188
    Roslyn Heights, New York 11577

Bill Muster
    Distributed by Rand McNally & Company

Nagel Publishers
   Distributed in the U.S.A. by Hippocrene Books, Inc.

National Directory Service, Inc.
   252 Ludlow Avenue
   Cincinnati, Ohio 45220

The New American Library, Inc.
   120 Woodbine Street
   Bergenfield, New Jersey 07621

Rail-Europe
   P.O. Box 3255
   Alexandria, Virginia 22302

Rand McNally & Company
   P.O. Box 7600
   Chicago, Illinois 60680

Random House
   201 E. 50th Street
   New York, New York 10022

St. Martin's Press, Inc.
   175 5th Avenue
   New York, New York 10010

Saltzman Companies
   27450 Pacific Coast Highway
   Malibu, California 90265

Charles Scribner's Sons
   597 5th Avenue
   New York, New York 10017

Simon & Schuster
   1230 Avenue of the Americas
   New York, New York 10020

Robert Speller & Sons, Publishers, Inc.
10 East 23rd Street
New York, New York 10010

Stackpole Books
Cameron & Keller Streets
Harrisburg, Pennsylvania 17105

Standing Orders, Inc.
P.O. Box 183
Patterson, New York 12563

Swiss Student Travel Office
Distributed by Council on International Educational Exchange

Trade and Travel Publications
Distirubted by Rand McNally & Company

Charles E. Tuttle Company, Inc.
28 S. Main Street
Rutland, Vermont 05701

Vacation-Work
9 Park End Street
Oxford, England
Distributed in the U.S.A. by National Directory Service, Inc.

Volunteers in Asia, Inc.
Distributed by Charles E. Tuttle Company, Inc.

Wexas International Limited
Distributed in the U.S.A. by World Expeditionary Association, North American Office, Graybar Building, Suite 354,
420 Lexington Avenue, New York, New York 10017

APPENDIX III
Guidebooks Published in Series

This appendix does not list the North American guides published in these series.

A to Z Guides
  Africa A to Z
  Asia A to Z
  Eastern Europe A to Z
  Grand Tour A to Z: The Capitals of Europe
  Italy A to Z: A Grand Tour of the Classic Cities
  London A to Z
  Paris A to Z

Arthur Frommer's Guides
  Athens
  Ireland/Dublin/Shannon
  Lisbon/Madrid/Costa del Sol
  London
  Paris
  Rome

APPENDIX III

Berlitz Travel Guides
    Amsterdam
    Athens
    Canary Islands
    Corfu
    Costa Brava
    Costa del Sol and Andalusia
    Costa Dorado and Barcelona
    Crete
    Dubrovnik and Southern Dalmatia
    Florence
    Ibiza and Formentera
    Istria and Croatian Coast
    Leningrad
    Loire Valley
    London
    Madeira
    Madrid
    Majorca and Minorca
    Moscow
    Rhodes
    Rome and the Vatican
    Split and Dalmatia
    Venice

Blue Guides
    The Adriatic Coast
    Athens and Environs
    Belgium and Luxembourg
    Bernese Oberland
    Crete
    Denmark
    England
    Greece
    Holland
    Ireland
    London
    Lucerne
    Malta

Northern Italy
Northwestern France
Paris
Rome and Environs
Scotland
Southern Italy
Southern Spain
South of France
Wales
Yugoslavia

Dollar Wise Guides
England
France
Germany
Italy
Portugal

Fodor's Guides
Australia, New Zealand & the South Pacific
Austria
Belgium and Luxembourg
Carribean, Bahamas, and Bermuda
Cruises Everywhere
Czechoslovakia
Egypt
Europe
Europe on a Budget
Europe Talking
France
Germany
Great Britain
Greece
Holland
Hungary
India
Iran
Ireland
Israel

Italy
Japan and Korea
London
Mexico
Morocco
Paris
Peking
Portugal
Railways of the World
Scandinavia
South America
Southeast Asia
Soviet Union
Spain
Switzerland
Tunisia
Turkey
Venice
Vienna
Yugoslavia

Holiday Travel Guides
Britain
The Caribbean and the Bahamas
France
Greece and the Aegean Islands
Ireland
Israel
Italy
London
Mexico
Paris
Rome
Scandinavia
Spain
West Germany

Lonely Planet Publications
Across Asia on the Cheap

Africa on the Cheap
Australia: A Traveller's Survival Kit
Nepal: A Traveller's Guide
New Zealand: A Travel Survival Kit
South-East Asia on a Shoestring
Trekking in the Himalayas

Michelin Green Guides (English Editions)
Austria
Brittany
Chateaux of the Loire
Dordogne
French Riveria
Germany
Italy
Normandy
Paris
Portugal
Spain
Switzerland

Michelin Red Gudies
Benelux
Camping in France
France
Germany
Great Britain and Ireland
Italy
London
Paris-English
Paris-French
Spain and Portugal

Nagel's Encyclopedia-Guides
Algeria
Austria
Balearic Islands
Bulgaria

Ceylon
Chateaux of the Loire
China
Cyprus
Czechoslovakia
Denmark-Greenland
Egypt
Finland
French and Italian Riveria
Germany (Federal Republic)
Great Britain and Ireland
Greece
Gulf Emirates
Holland
Hungary
Iceland
India and Nepal
Iran
Israel
Italy
Japan
Leningrad and its Environs
Malta
Mexico
Morocco
Moscow and its Environs
Poland
Portugal (Madeira, the Azores)
Rome
Rumania
Spain
Sweden
Thailand, Angkor (Cambodia)
Turkey
USSR
Yugoslavia

Sunset Travel Guides
- *Australia*
- *Europe: Discovery Trips*
- *Islands of the South Pacific*
- *Japan*
- *Mexico*
- *New Zealand*
- *The Orient*
- *Southeast Asia*

$10-a-Day Guides
- *England on $15 a Day*
- *Europe on $10 a Day*
- *Greece on $10 a Day*
- *India (plus Sri Lanka and Nepal) on $5 & $10 a Day*
- *Ireland on $10 a Day*
- *Israel on $10 & $15 a Day*
- *Mexico and Guatemala on $10 a Day*
- *New Zealand on $10 a Day*
- *Scandinavia on $15 & $20 a Day*
- *South America on $10 & $15 a Day*
- *Spain and Morocco (plus the Canary Islands) on $10 & $15 a Day*
- *Turkey on $5 & $10 a Day*

Appendix IV
Basic Travel Library

The World
    Overlanding: How to Explore the World on Four Wheels $4.95
    The 1978 Student Travel Catalog   free
    Whole World Handbook: A Student Guide to Work, Study and Travel Abroad $3.95

Europe
    Europe on $10 a Day $4.95
    Eurail Guide: How to Travel Europe by Train $5.95
    International Youth Hostel Handbook, Volume I: Europe and Mediterranean Countries $3.25
    Let's Go: The Budget Guide to Europe $4.95
    Student Hostels and Tour Activities: Handbook for the Young Traveler $1.00

Africa
> *Africa on the Cheap* $3.95
> *The Traveler's Africa* $14.95

Asia
> *All-Asia Guide* $5.95
> *The On-Your-Own Guide to Asia* $3.95
> *The Student Guide to Asia* $3.95

South America
> *The South American Handbook* $16.95
> *The Student Guide to Latin America* $2.95

> The guidebook with information on all the books you are unable to afford:

Travel Guidebooks in Review $9.95

TOTAL LIBRARY $91.60

> Note: All of these books except *The 1978 Student Travel Catalog* and *Travel Guidebooks in Review* are reviewed in this book and are available from the publisher listed in the review. *The Student Travel Catalog* is a free pamphlet available from CIEE, 777 United Nations Plaza, New York, New York 10017

Appendix V

Basic Study Abroad Library

General Directories
    *The New Guide to Study Abroad
        Available from Harper & Row $5.95
    *Whole World Handbook
        Available from CIEE $3.95

Listings of Specific Programs
    **Summer Study Abroad $5.00
    **U.S. College Sponsored Programs Abroad: Academic Year $5.00

Books On Specific Geographic Areas and Fields
    **Handbook on International Study for U.S. Nationals: Study in Europe $6.95

**Handbook on International Study for U.S. Nationals:
 Study in the American Republics Area $6.95
African Colleges and Universities $3.75
 Available from the African American Institute
 833 U.N. Plaza, New York, New York 10017
**Guide to Foreign Medical Schools $5.00

Scholarships
 Study Abroad $7.50
 Available from Unipub, Box 433, New York, New York 10016

"How To"
 SECUSSA Sourcebook: A Guide for Advisors of U.S. Students Planning an Overseas Experience $4.00
 Available from NAFSA, 1860 19th St., N.W. Washington, D.C. 20009

TOTAL LIBRARY $54.05

*Complete addresses can be found in the publishers and distributors listing, appendix II.

**Available from the Institute of International Education, 809 U.N. Plaza, New York, New York 10017

Appendix VI
Basic International Employment Library

General Directories
    Career Opportunities in the International Field $3.50
      Available from the School of Foreign Service,
      Georgetown University, Washington, D.C. 20057
    *Whole World Handbook: A Student Guide to Work,
      Study and Travel Abroad* $3.95
      Available from CIEE

Short-Term Nonprofessional Employment
    The Directory of Overseas Summer Jobs $6.95
      Available from Gaylord Professional Publications
    Emplois D'Ete En France $4.95
      Available from CIEE
    The 1978 Student Travel Catalog free
      Available from CIEE
    Summer Jobs in Britain $5.95
      Available from Gaylord Professional Publications

Volunteer Opportunities
  Invest Yourself $2.00
    Available from LAOS/ASF, Circulation Department 418 Peltoma Road Haddonfield, New Jersey 08033.

Teaching
  Teaching Abroad $4.00
    Available from IEE, 809 United Nations Plaza, New York, New York 10017.

Government*
  Federal Jobs Overseas $.30
    Available from Superintendent of Documents, U.S. Government Printing Office, Washington, D.C. 20402.

Business*

International Organizations*

Law
  Directory of Opportunities in International Law $4.00
    Available from Publications Committee, J.B. Moore
    Society of International Law, School of Law, University of Virginia, Charlottesville, Virginia 22901.

TOTAL LIBRARY $35.60

*Information for these areas is contained in *Career Opportunities in the International Field*, available from the School of Foreign Service, Georgetown University, Washington, D.C. 20057